Soviet economic
development from
Lenin to Khrushchev

Important
chapter 4

p25 famine + 29 30

Death² 50, 63  70

Famine — 22 25 64
     2,45 48 50 54
Food — 64
     20 23 27 39 40 45 54 63
Requistioning 21
     74
supply 16 20 30 5 25 +              grain
grain 48 57 60 9 27 29   Crisis
14 15  23 41 66 69 71    — 31-23 34 36
Requistioning 18 20 23

# New Studies in Economic and Social History

*Edited for the Economic History Society by*
Michael Sanderson
*University of East Anglia, Norwich*

This series, specially commissioned by the Economic History Society, provides a guide to the current interpretations of the key themes of economic and social history in which advances have recently been made or in which there has been significant debate.

In recent times economic and social history has been one of the most flourishing areas of historical study. This has mirrored the increasing relevance of the economic and social sciences both in a student's choice of career and in forming a society at large more aware of the importance of these issues in their everyday lives. Moreover specialist interests in business, agricultural and welfare history, for example, have themselves burgeoned and there has been an increased interest in the economic development of the wider world. Stimulating as these scholarly developments have been for the specialist, the rapid advance of the subject and the quantity of new publications make it difficult for the reader to gain an overview of particular topics, let alone the whole field.

*New Studies in Economic and Social History* is intended for students and their teachers. It is designed to introduce them to fresh topics and to enable them to keep abreast of recent writing and debates. All the books in the series are written by a recognised authority in the subject, and the arguments and issues are set out in a critical but unpartisan fashion. The aim of the series is to survey the current state of scholarship, rather than to provide a set of pre-packaged conclusions.

The series has been edited since its inception in 1968 by Professors M. W. Flinn, T. C. Smout and L. A. Clarkson, and is currently edited by Dr Michael Sanderson. From 1968 it was published by Macmillan as *Studies in Economic History*, and after 1974 as *Studies in Economic and Social History*. From 1995 *New Studies in Economic and Social History* is being published on behalf of the Economic History Society by Cambridge University Press. This new series includes some of the titles previously published by Macmillan as well as new titles, and reflects the ongoing development throughout the world of this rich seam of history.

*For a full list of titles in print, please see the end of the book.*

# Soviet economic development from Lenin to Khrushchev

*Prepared for the Economic History Society by*

R. W. Davies
*University of Birmingham*

PUBLISHED BY THE PRESS SYNDICATE OF THE UNIVERSITY OF CAMBRIDGE
The Pitt Building, Trumpington Street, Cambridge CB2 1RP, United
Kingdom

CAMBRIDGE UNIVERSITY PRESS
The Edinburgh Building, Cambridge CB2 2RU, United Kingdom
40 West 20th Street, New York, NY 10011–4211, USA
10 Stamford Road, Oakleigh, Melbourne 3166, Australia

First published 1998

Printed in the United Kingdom at the University Press, Cambridge

Typeset in 10/12½ pt Plantin    [CE]

*A catalogue record for this book is available from the British Library*

ISBN 0 521 62260 3 hardback
ISBN 0 521 62742 7 paperback

# Contents

| | | |
|---|---|---|
| *List of maps* | *page* | vi |
| *List of figures* | | vi |
| *List of tables* | | vii |
| *Acknowledgements* | | viii |
| *Main dates in Russian and Soviet history* | | ix |
| *Glossary* | | xi |

| | | |
|---|---|---|
| 1 | Introduction | 1 |
| 2 | The Tsarist economy | 6 |
| 3 | War Communism, 1918–1920 | 17 |
| 4 | The New Economic Policy of the 1920s | 23 |
| 5 | Measuring Soviet economic growth | 38 |
| 6 | Soviet economic development, 1928–1965 | 43 |
| | The pre-war industrialisation drive, 1928–1941 | 43 |
| | The Second World War, 1941–1945 | 58 |
| | Post-war recovery, 1945–1950 | 64 |
| | Post-war expansion, 1950–1965 | 67 |
| 7 | The Soviet economic system, 1928–1965 | 73 |
| 8 | Soviet industrialisation in perspective | 79 |

| | |
|---|---|
| *Further reading* | 83 |
| *References* | 85 |
| *Index* | 92 |

# Maps and figures

**Maps**
1 Republics, cities and major towns of the
  USSR at the end of the 1930s    *page* xvi
2 Agricultural regions of the USSR
  (including the Virgin Lands)    xviii
3 Industrial regions of the USSR    xx

**Figure**
1 Agricultural and industrial prices, 1922–5,
  illustrating the 'scissors crisis' of 1923    *page* 28

# Tables

| | | | |
|---|---|---|---|
| 1 | Gross national product, 1928 and 1937 | *page* | 39 |
| 2 | Gross national product by end-use, 1928 and 1937 | | 40 |
| 3 | Index of munitions output, 1940–4 | | 41 |
| 4 | Gross national product, 1928–60 | | 42 |
| 5 | Western pre-*glasnost'* estimates of camp population | | 49 |
| 6 | Total number of prisoners in the forced labour system | | 49 |
| 7 | Gross national product by sector of origin, 1940–5 | | 60 |
| 8 | Defence outlays as percentage of GDP, 1940–4 | | 61 |
| 9 | Gross military and civil industrial production, 1940–7 | | 65 |
| 10 | Gross national product by sector of origin, 1928–65 | | 82 |
| 11 | Non-agricultural employment by sector of the economy, 1928–65 | | 82 |

# Acknowledgements

I am most grateful to Peter Gatrell, Mark Harrison, Michael Sanderson (the Editor of this series), Robert Service and Stephen Wheatcroft for their many helpful comments and suggestions on the first draft of the typescript, to Melanie Ilič for preparation of the index and assistance with the maps, and to Yvonne Hall for secretarial assistance. Much of the research on which this book is based was financed by the Economic and Social Science Research Council, and assisted by the Centre for Russian and European Studies of the University of Birmingham and its Alexander Baykov Library. I have drawn extensively on our fuller collective study, R. W. Davies, M. Harrison and S. G. Wheatcroft (eds.), *The Economic Transformation of the Soviet Union, 1913–1945*, Cambridge, 1994.

# Main dates in Russian and Soviet history

| | | |
|---|---|---|
| 988 | | Adoption of Christianity by Kievan Rus' |
| 1240–1380 | | Mongol domination of Russia |
| 1533–84 | | Reign of Ivan IV ('the Terrible') |
| 1694–1725 | | Reign of Peter I ('the Great') |
| 1861 | | Emancipation of serf peasantry |
| 1890s | | First industrialisation drive |
| 1905 | | First Russian revolution |
| 1906 | | First Duma elected on limited franchise |
| 1906–11 | | Stolypin's agrarian reforms |
| 1909–13 | | Industrial boom |
| 1914 | July | Outbreak of First World War |
| 1917 | February/March | Liberal-democratic revolution overthrows Tsar; establishment of Provisional Government |
| 1917 | October/ November | Bolshevik ('October') revolution |
| 1918–20 | | Civil War; 'War Communism' |
| 1921–9 | | New Economic Policy |
| 1924 | 21 January | Death of Lenin |
| 1926–8 | | Pre-1914 industrial and agricultural output restored |
| 1927–8 | Winter | Grain crisis |
| 1928 (Oct.)– 1932 (Dec.) | | First five-year plan |
| 1929 | Autumn | Defeat of Bukharin group |

| 1929 | End of year | Mass collectivisation of agriculture and 'dekulakisation' begin |
| 1932–3 | | Widespread famine |
| 1933 | January | Hitler appointed Chancellor of German Reich |
| 1933–7 | | Second five-year plan |
| 1935 | | End of food rationing |
| 1936–8 | | 'Great Purge'; execution of Bukharin, military leader Tukhachevsky and others |
| 1938–42 | | Third five-year plan (interrupted by German invasion) |
| 1939 | 23 August | Soviet–German Pact |
| 1941 | 22 June | Nazi Germany invades USSR |
| 1941 | October | Moscow under siege |
| 1942 | November | Soviet victory at Stalingrad |
| 1945 | 9 May | Victory over Germany |
| 1946–50 | | Fourth five-year plan |
| 1949 | | Pre-war gross national product restored |
| 1953 | 5 March | Death of Stalin |
| 1956 | February | XXth Party Congress: Khrushchev denounces Stalin |
| 1964 | 14 October | Khrushchev dismissed; replaced as First (General) Secretary of Party by Brezhnev |
| 1985 | March | Gorbachev appointed General Secretary of Party |
| 1991 | December | Soviet Union dissolved |

# Glossary

| | |
|---|---|
| Bolsheviks | more revolutionary section, headed by Lenin, of Russian Social Democratic Labour Party (so-called from the Russian *bol'shinstvo*, majority, because they obtained a majority of votes at one stage in the 1903 Congress) |
| bourgeoisie (capitalist class) | in Marxist theory, the class that owns the means of production and exploits the working class under capitalism |
| communism | in Marxist theory, in the higher stage of communism, when goods are abundant, means of production will be publicly owned as under socialism (q.v.), but distribution will be according to the principle 'from each according to ability, to each according to need', not according to work done |
| Donbass | Donets coal basin |
| Duma | pre-revolutionary parliament with limited powers and franchise, established 1906; the |

| | |
|---|---|
| | same name is used for the new Russian parliament established in 1993 |
| excess deaths | premature deaths due to famine, violence or epidemics |
| GNP | gross national product |
| Gorbachev, M. S. | (b. 1931) General Secretary of the Communist Party of the Soviet Union, 1985–91 |
| Gosplan (Gosudarstvennaya planovaya komissiya) | State Planning Commission |
| gross production | total output of goods by an economic unit (including inputs to the unit) |
| Gulag (Glavnoe upravlenie lagerei) | Chief Administration of Corrective Labour Camps |
| industry (*promyshlennost'*) | mining and manufacturing industry (Russian term excludes building industry, transport, etc.) |
| infant mortality | annual death rate in first year of life, per 1,000 live births |
| KGB (Komitet gosudarstvennoi bezopasnosti) | Committee of State Security (post-war successor to NKVD) |
| Khrushchev, N. S. | (1894–1971) First (General) Secretary of the Communist Party of the Soviet Union, 1953–64 |
| *kolkhoz* (pl. *kolkhozy*) | collective farm |
| *kulak* | more prosperous peasant (Russian word for 'closed fist' or 'tight fist') |
| large-scale industry (*krupnaya promyshlennost'*) | normally included industrial units employing 16 workers or |

| | |
|---|---|
| | more when using mechanical power, or 30 workers or more otherwise; all other industry was classified as 'small-scale' |
| Lenin, V. I. | (1870–1924) leader of Bolsheviks before and after October 1917 revolution |
| Marx, Karl | (1818–83) Founder of scientific communism |
| MTS (*mashino-traktornaya stantsiya*) | Machine-Tractor Station |
| NEP (*novaya ekonomicheskaya politika*) | New Economic Policy |
| NKVD (Narodnyi komissariat vnutrennikh del) | People's Commissariat (equivalent to Ministry) of Internal Affairs (formerly responsible for political police) |
| NNP | net national product (GNP less depreciation) |
| Politburo | political committee of Central Committee of Communist Party, effectively supreme centre of power |
| ruble (*rubl'*) | unit of Russian/Soviet currency |
| socialism | in Marxist theory, the first or lower stage of communism; factories, mines and other means of production are publicly owned, and distribution is on the principle 'from each according to ability, to each according to work done' |
| soviet | Russian word for council, originally the name of local revolutionary bodies elected by |

| | |
|---|---|
| | workers, soldiers and peasants; until 1993 the name of central and local government organs |
| Soviet Union | *see* USSR |
| Stalin, I. V. | (1879–1953) General Secretary of Communist Party 1922–53, dominant political leader from about 1928 |
| tonnes | Tonnes (metric tons) are used throughout this book. 1 tonne = 2204.6 lb. |
| Trotsky, L. D. | (1879–1940) Soviet revolutionary leader, headed Left Opposition from 1923, expelled from USSR 1929, murdered 1940 |
| USSR (SSSR – Soyuz sovetskikh sotsialisticheskikh respublik) | Union of Soviet Socialist Republics, inaugurated in 1922; by 1941 had sixteen constituent republics; dissolved December 1991 |

ARCTIC

WHITE
SEA

*Murmansk*

BALTIC SEA

ESTONIA
LITHU-
ANIA
LATVIA
*Leningrad* *Lake Ladoga*
*Arkhangel'sk*
*Novgorod*

BELORUSSIA
*Minsk* *Smolensk* *Kalinin*
*L'vov*
*Yaroslavl'*
*Moscow* *Ivanovo*
*Vyaz'ma*
*Kiev* *Orel* *Tula* *Gor'kii* *Kirov*
MOLDAVIA
UKRAINE *Kursk*
*Odessa* *Khar'kov* *Kazan'* *Perm'*
*Poltava* *Voronezh*
*Zaporozh'e* *Penza*
CRIMEA *Mariupol'* *Donetsk* *Kuznetsk* *Pervoural'sk* *Nizhnii Tagil*
*Lugansk* *Kuibyshev* *Sverdlovsk*
*Sevastopol'* Sea of *Rostov-* *Stalingrad* *Chelyabinsk*
*Kerch* Azov *on-Don* *Magnitogorsk*
BLACK SEA *Krasnodar* *Orenburg* *Omsk*
NORTH CAUCASUS *Novo*
*Kislovodsk*
*Mozdok*

URAL MOUNTAINS

RUSSIAN SO

KAZAKHSTAN
*Karaganda*

GEORGIA
ARMENIA
AZER-
BAIJAN
*Baku*

CASPIAN SEA

*Aral
Sea*
*Lake Balkhash*

*Krasnovodsk*
TURKMENIA

UZBEKISTAN

KIRGIZIA

TADZHIKISTAN

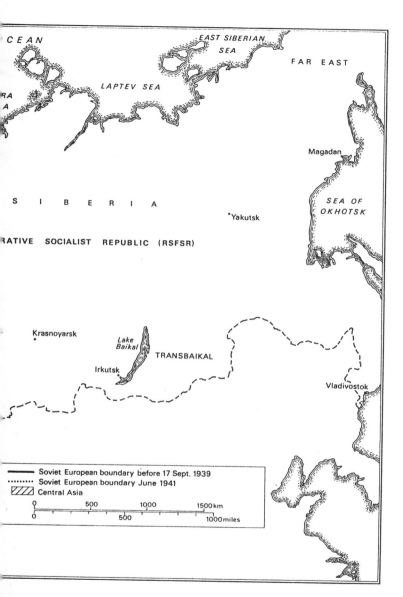

C E A N

EAST SIBERIAN SEA

FAR EAST

LAPTEV SEA

RA
A

Magadan

S    I    B    E    R    I    A

SEA OF OKHOTSK

•Yakutsk

RATIVE   SOCIALIST   REPUBLIC   (RSFSR)

Krasnoyarsk
•

Lake
Baikal

TRANSBAIKAL

Irkutsk
•

Vladivostok

Soviet European boundary before 17 Sept. 1939
Soviet European boundary June 1941
Central Asia

| 0 | | 500 | | 1000 | | 1500 km |
| 0 | | | 500 | | | 1000 miles |

*Map 1* Republics, cities and major towns of the USSR at the end of the
930s

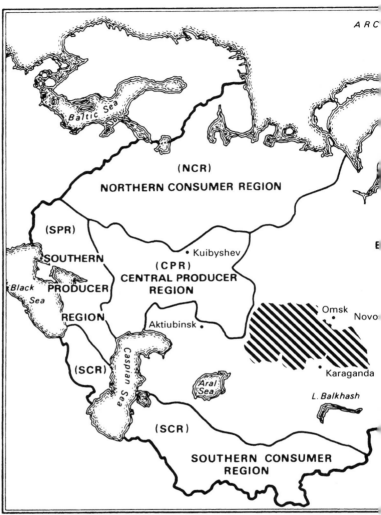

*Map 2* Agricultural regions of the USSR (including the Virgin Lands).
The Russian Empire and the Soviet Union were conventionally divide[d]
into grain-surplus and grain-deficit regions, known as 'producer' an[d]
'consumer' regions, respectively. The three producer regions supplie[d]
grain to the consumer regions and for export. These were:

    *Central Producer Region (CPR)* Central Black-Earth, Volga and
    South-East;
    *Southern Producer Region (SPR)* Ukraine and Southern Steppe;
    *Eastern Producer Region (EPR)* Urals, Siberia and Kazakhstan.
The two consumer regions were net importers of grain:

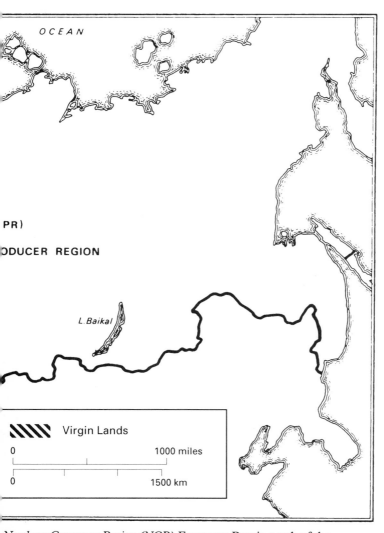

OCEAN

PR)

ODUCER REGION

L.Baikal

◤◤◤◤ Virgin Lands

0                   1000 miles

0                   1500 km

*Northern Consumer Region (NCR)* European Russia north of the
SPR and CPR;
*Southern Consumer Region (SCR)* Transcaucasus and Central Asia.
or further details see Wheatcroft and Davies 1994c, pp. 108–9, 111.
he Virgin Lands of North Kazakhstan and Siberia were developed for
tensive grain production between 1954 and 1960 (see p. 69). The map
ows the central Virgin Lands region in North Kazakhstan. In addition,
used lands in southern Siberia adjacent to North Kazakhstan, in the
rals, in the North Caucasus and elsewhere were brought into cultivation
ring the Virgin Lands campaign.

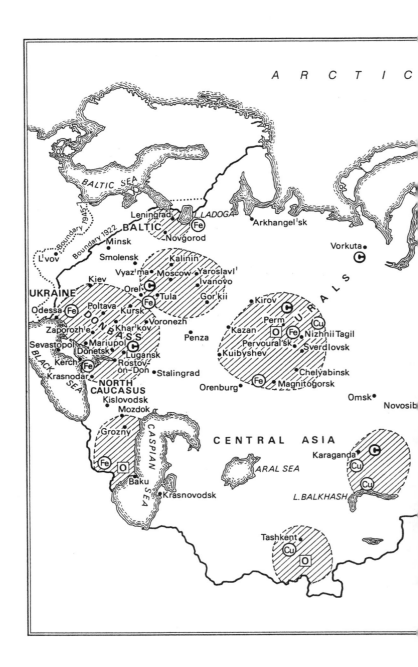

*Map 3* Industrial regions of the USSR.

# 1
# Introduction

The Russian Empire of the Tsars, which was overthrown in 1917, and its successor the Soviet Union, which disintegrated in 1991, were by far the largest states in the world, occupying 15 per cent of the world's land surface, nearly a hundred times the area of Great Britain. They embraced every kind of soil and climate, from the permanently frozen Arctic to the Central Asian tropics. Most of the country experiences a harsh continental climate; the main agricultural areas are at the latitude of Canada and the northern United States, and the severe conditions result in a very wide annual variation in yields.

Between the fifteenth and the nineteenth centuries the Russian rulers gradually established their authority over this vast territory from their small initial base in the Moscow region. By 1900 Russians amounted to a little more than half the total population; and other Slavs to a further 20 per cent. More than a hundred non-Slav languages were spoken by the Caucasians, the Turkic and Iranian peoples, the Balts and others who constituted the remaining one-third of the population.

In the course of the first half of the twentieth century the Russian Empire/USSR was transformed from a predominantly agrarian country into a major industrial power. In this economic transformation Russia in many respects followed the path of its predecessors Britain, France, Germany and the United States. But the bumpy Russian road to industrialisation was unique in several important respects.

First, *war and revolution*, and their social and political consequences, overshadowed and distorted economic development to an extent unprecedented in nineteenth-century Europe. The direct effect on the economy of the Russo-Japanese War (1904–5) and the unsuccessful 1905–6 revolution was relatively minor. Although industrial growth was held up for a few years, it resumed in 1908. But between 1914 and 1920, world war, the two 1917 revolutions and the Civil War resulted in a catastrophic fall in production from which the economy did not recover until about 1927. Then, during the devastating German invasion of 1941–5, most of the major industrial regions were occupied by the enemy; and industrial production did not recover to its 1940 level until about 1949. So in the first sixty years of this century there were only thirty-seven years of 'normal' economic development (1900–3, 1907–14, 1928–40, 1949–60). And even in these 'normal' years, fear of war, and actual rearmament, influenced the pattern of economic development to a greater extent than in the case of the other major powers.

The two world wars and the Civil War resulted in far greater population losses than in other countries. Population losses (also known as the population deficit) consist, first, of *excess deaths*, which are premature deaths due to violence, famine or epidemic, and, secondly, of the *birth deficit*, which is the loss in population due to a temporary fall in the birth rate. It has been estimated that the First World War and the Civil War resulted in 16 million excess deaths from violence, hunger and disease, and a birth deficit of a further 10 million; and during the Second World War excess deaths reached as many as 26 to 27 million, and the birth deficit amounted to a further 12 million or so. Stalinist industrialisation also led to a large number of peacetime excess deaths, perhaps ten million or more, many of them during the famine of 1933. Thus the total population loss in the period 1914–45 from both premature deaths and the birth deficit amounted to over 74 million persons (26 million in 1914–22, 38 million in 1941–5, 10 million or more in peacetime years). Historians continue to debate how far the social upheaval and human suffering were integral to Soviet economic development, and how far they should be looked upon as extraneous events.

Secondly, *pre-revolutionary Russia*, even at the end of the nineteenth century, had important *characteristics in common with the great Asiatic states – India and China*. More than 80 per cent of the population lived in the countryside; the land was cultivated by over 20 million peasant householders, and over 90 per cent of the cultivated area was sown to grain. Straddling Europe and Asia, Russia presented a dual face to the world: a colonial power and a semi-colony; the most backward of the European powers, and the most advanced of the great peasant countries. And Tsarist and Stalinist industrialisation was not merely the industrialisation of a European power but also the first case of the rapid industrialisation of a peasant country within a few decades.

Thirdly, *the active role played by the state* was also without precedent. Alexander Gerschenkron argued that in the second half of the nineteenth century, with Britain already in place as an industrial power, other European nations could overcome their 'economic backwardness' only if their governments created 'substitutes' for the free market which would temporarily provide adequate incentives for industrial development. Thus in Imperial Germany import tariffs were imposed by the state, and national banks were created under the influence of the state. In pre-revolutionary Russia the state played an even more active role in encouraging industrialisation (Gerschenkron 1965). But the pre-revolutionary Russian state had far wider functions and ambitions. Over many centuries successive tsars sought actively, if intermittently, to strengthen Russian economic and military might in their endeavour to establish the Russian Empire as a great power equal with its more prosperous European neighbours. And in the Soviet Union from the 1930s onwards the state was much more powerful. It owned nearly the whole of industry and large-scale trade, and sought to manage the economy by a comprehensive central plan. State socialism was seen not as a mere device to encourage industrialisation but as an alternative and superior system which would come to replace private capitalism throughout the world.

Four economic systems, in all of which the state played a crucial role, succeeded one another in the twentieth century:

*The Tsarist economy,* with its state-influenced market – including the 1914–7 wartime variant in which state regulation was intensified;

*'War Communism'* (1918–20) – a thoroughgoing attempt at state ownership and management of a moneyless economy in kind, supplemented in practice by illegal private trade and barter;

The period of the *New Economic Policy* (1921–9), a mixed economy in which state-owned industry and private peasant agriculture co-operated and competed through the market;

*The 'administrative economy'*, established in the early 1930s, which continued with modifications until the collapse of the Communist system in 1991. Production and investment in state-owned industry, and a collective agriculture under close state control, were administered largely through physical controls from the centre. Contrary to what is commonly assumed, central planning was supplemented by informal horizontal relations between enterprises, and by important market or quasi-market features which were essential to the operation of the economy. This system, at first described in the West as the 'Great Experiment' in state planning, seemed by the end of the Second World War to have succeeded in establishing itself as the main rival to Western capitalism. Even at the time of the launching of Gorbachev's reforms in 1985 hardly anyone – inside or outside the Soviet Union – anticipated its collapse. The reasons for the fall of the Soviet regime and its economic system will long be debated.

In the following pages many figures will be cited to illustrate and assess economic development. The difficulties involved in establishing the main quantitative features of economic growth are familiar to all students of economic history. Yet before 1917 Russian national and regional statistics were relatively well-developed, far fuller and more reliable than the statistics for Britain in the early nineteenth century. After the October revolution, detailed and reliable statistics were published until the end of the 1920s. But we shall see that even with this strong statistical base many fundamental issues remain contentious. Did peasant prosperity increase or decrease in the decades before 1914? Did the state role in industry increase or decline on the eve of the world war? And the break in administration following the revolution has made reliable comparisons of the pre- and post-revolutionary economies particularly difficult.

From 1930 onwards Soviet economic statistics confront us with major new problems. First, the rate of change, particularly in the capital goods industries, makes an 'objective' statement about the rate of industrial growth extremely difficult. Secondly, the quantity and range of published statistics greatly diminished after 1930, and particularly in the later 1930s; many series are only now becoming available in the archives, and others were not collected at all. Thirdly, the Soviet authorities deliberately distorted their published statistics in order to present a more favourable impression of economic progress. The grain harvest was falsified; population data were partly concealed, partly falsified; the success of the consumer goods industries was exaggerated. All this has made it particularly necessary to pay attention to the reliability of our statistical base in describing Soviet economic development; chapter 5 examines these questions.

# 2

# The Tsarist economy

The power of the tsars over their multi-national empire was exercised through the creation of a centralised state. From the sixteenth century onwards they sought intermittently to establish Russia as a great European power. But Russia was economically and socially less advanced than her rivals; and successive tsars sought to strengthen her economic and military might. Peter the Great (1694–1725) used serf labour on a large scale to construct from scratch the Western-style capital St Petersburg on the Baltic (known as Petrograd in the period 1914–24, and Leningrad in the period 1924–91). He also used serf labour to build up a charcoal-based iron industry, largely for military purposes, in the Urals on the borders of Europe and Asia.

During the early nineteenth century, the Russian market widened considerably, and a cotton-based textile industry developed rapidly, largely using imported machinery from Britain. The growth of the internal market occurred in spite of the continuance of serfdom in Russia longer than in the rest of Europe. Perhaps the most important event in Russian nineteenth-century history was the liberation of the serfs by Alexander II's Emancipation Act of 1861. Peasant emancipation paved the way for further economic development. It was now easier for former serfs to participate in the market – and even essential for them to do so, as they had to earn money by selling products on the market, or by selling their labour, in order to pay the high redemption charges imposed by the 1861 Act.

Historians used to argue that the main economic consequence of the Act was to free labour for employment in industry: industrial labour was scarce before 1861 because the peasants were tied to the land. But Crisp has shown that abundant labour was potentially available before 1861 (Crisp 1978). Baykov forcefully argues that it was not labour shortage but the unfortunate location of resources which hindered industrial growth. Population and industrial skills were concentrated in the central area of European Russia around Moscow and St Petersburg; coking coal and iron ore were located in the south, and transport in a northerly direction by river was impossible. Development of the railways with state support and regulation in the 1870s and 1880s was the prerequisite for 'modern' industrialisation based on the coke-smelting of iron (Baykov 1954, pp. 137–49).

The industrial boom of the 1890s, during which large-scale industrial production increased by as much as 8–9 per cent a year, launched Russia into the age of heavy industry. Von Laue's study of Finance Minister Witte shows how he persuaded the reluctant Nicholas II that state-encouraged industrialisation was essential if the Russian autocracy was to remain a political force in the modern age (Von Laue 1963). Witte, building on the work of his predecessors in the finance ministry, introduced the gold standard, supported high import tariffs, arranged state finance and support for the expanding railway network, and encouraged foreign investment in Russian industry. This was the fourth occasion (following Petrine industrialisation, serf emancipation and railway construction) in which the state played a major role in encouraging economic development. Russian economic history up to 1900 was the story of how market-led and state-induced development complemented and competed with each other.

The iron and steel industry provides the most striking example of the role of the state. The main consumers of iron and steel were the railways, which were built in accordance with a state-managed plan. The state guaranteed foreign loans for railway construction, and provided substantial sums for railway construction from the budget. From the end of the 1870s it also actively encouraged the production of rails and rolling stock by Russian industry. The state provided the infant railway engineering industry with substantial orders, and in 1877 high tariffs were imposed on imports of rails and rolling stock. Foreign companies were encouraged by the state to invest in the iron and steel industry. The production of pig-iron increased from 350,000 tonnes in 1870 to 2,700,000 tonnes in

1899. By the end of the 1890s nearly 60 per cent of all iron and steel was consumed by the railways (Gatrell 1986, pp. 150–4).

In contrast, the cotton textile industry was almost entirely market-led. Cotton textiles purchased by the state were negligible, and, in contrast to the iron, coal and other capital goods industries, almost all capital invested in the industry was Russian-owned.

Industrialisation had begun to link the Russian economy firmly with the world market; and the boom of the 1890s was followed by an industrial depression in 1899–1902, in common with the rest of Europe. The depression was particularly severe in Russia, because it coincided with a reduction in state orders for the railways.

Industrialisation was accompanied by growing political and social instability. The humiliating defeat in the war with Japan (1904–5) was certainly one of the factors which triggered the outbreak of the 1905 revolution. But the fundamental causes of the revolution lay far deeper. Discontent was widespread among the new classes which had emerged with the growth of industry and the towns: factory workers were dissatisfied with their economic and social conditions; the urban middle class were demanding political rights. And the discontent spread to large sections of the peasantry.

The 1905 revolution was brought to an end by coercion and concession. The Tsar permitted the establishment of a state Duma (parliament) on a very restricted and unequal franchise, and with limited powers. And following the revolution the state embarked in 1907 on its fifth major endeavour to encourage economic development: the agrarian reforms of Prime Minister Peter A. Stolypin. At the beginning of the twentieth century most Russian peasant households lived in a village commune. The main arable fields were divided into strips, which were periodically redistributed among the households, and cultivated by the traditional three-field system. The Stolypin reforms encouraged peasants to leave the village commune and to establish separate holdings. Stolypin believed that individual holdings would provide greater economic incentives for the peasants and would create a prosperous yeoman class as a stable support for the government.

The Stolypin reforms were introduced in generally favourable economic conditions. With the end of the world agricultural depression, which had lasted from the mid-1870s to the end of the 1890s, international grain prices rose substantially from the beginning of the new century. Russian agricultural production increased in the period 1900–14. It is difficult to distinguish the effect of the Stolypin reforms themselves from the generally favourable conditions which led to the improvement of agricultural performance in the main grain regions.

Simultaneously with the Stolypin reforms, industry entered a new period of rapid growth, which continued until the outbreak of war in 1914 and through the first two years of war. Between 1908 and 1913, the production of large-scale industry increased by almost 8 per cent a year, nearly as rapidly as in the 1890s (Gregory 1996); small-scale industry (including seasonal production by peasant artisans) probably increased at a similar rate (Gatrell and Davies 1990, p. 129). National income as a whole grew by over 5 per cent a year (Davies 1990, p. 5). At this time the population was increasing by some 2.4 per cent a year, so production per head of population increased substantially.

By the eve of the First World War the Russian economy had undergone immense changes as compared with the situation at the time of the Emancipation Act of 1861. The production of large-scale industry in 1913 has been estimated at over eleven times the 1860 level. Large-scale manufacturing and mining employed some $2\frac{1}{2}$ million workers in 1913. In the market-led sector of industry, pride of place was occupied by cotton textiles, which by 1913 employed about 20 per cent of all workers in large-scale industry (most of them women). But the capital goods industries, especially fuel, iron and steel and machine building, expanded more rapidly than the consumer goods industries. (On pre-revolutionary industry, see Gatrell and Davies 1990.)

The capital goods industries, unlike the consumer goods industries, were largely foreign-owned, particularly by British, French and German capital; to a somewhat lesser extent they were also foreign-managed. And, following the 1899–1902 depression, in most of these industries, including iron and steel, coal, oil and railway engineering, 'syndicates' (*sindikaty*) were formed. The syndicates were the Russian equivalent of cartels. They decided on sales quotas for their member firms, and determined the wholesale prices. Thus capital goods industries, with some exceptions, were financed from abroad and under the strong influence of the state, and had marked oligopolistic tendencies.

In spite of the development of industry, Russia on the eve of the First World War was still primarily an agrarian peasant country. Agriculture was responsible for over half the national income, and three-quarters of all employment. Over 90 per cent of the sown area was cultivated by some 20 million peasant households, the remainder consisting of landowners' estates. Agricultural production expanded greatly after 1861, and the peasant economy was increasingly involved in the market. But a large part of peasant production of food, and to some extent of consumer goods, was consumed by the families which produced it, or by other families within the same village. The villages were still to a considerable extent self-sufficient. By 1914 the Stolypin reform had not affected most peasant households, which continued to farm as part of the village commune.

In the Tsarist economy, then, a number of economic structures co-existed: foreign-owned oligopolies in the capital goods industries, freely competing Russian firms producing consumer goods, landowners' estates, small-scale artisan units, and an immense number of individual peasant micro-economies. This was a market economy strongly influenced by the state, but in which most of the participants still themselves produced many of the goods which they consumed.

There is no agreed view among historians on either the systemic features or the dynamics of the Tsarist economy on the eve of the First World War. Gerschenkron argued that the economy entered a new phase after the 1905 revolution. Industrial development no longer depended on the state. According to Gerschenkron, the boom of 1908–13 was primarily due to an increase in consumer spending; the role of the state was declining. Russian capital and entrepreneurship were replacing foreign capital. The state-induced industrialisation of the 1890s had been transformed into the market-led progress of the capitalist economy of 1908–13 (Gerschenkron 1965).

On balance, the evidence does not confirm this view. It is true that the consumer goods industries expanded rapidly during the boom of 1908–13. But state orders increased equally rapidly, largely as a result of the huge expansion in defence expenditure (Gatrell 1982, pp. 104–5; Gatrell and Davies 1990, pp. 146–7). Nor is the relative role of Russian and foreign capital and entrepreneurship at all clear-cut. While the share of Russian capital and management was increasing in a number of well-established industries, foreign capital was dominant in new industries such as electrical engineering. Its overall role had probably not diminished.

There has been much discussion among Western economic historians about the role of the state in Russian economic development. Most historians would now agree that Gerschenkron and von Laue overestimated the extent to which the state pursued a coherent and systematic industrialisation programme. State tariff policy as a whole, for example, was determined by the need for budgetary revenue as well as the hope of developing Russian infant industries; tariffs were levied on the import of food products as well as industrial materials and manufactures. Nevertheless some specific tariffs certainly assisted Russian industry: as a result of the duty on pig-iron, which rose very rapidly between 1868 and 1891, and continued to prevail until 1917, iron produced in southern Russia was cheaper than imports (Kahan 1967, pp. 470–1; Gatrell 1986, pp. 165–7).

There is also wide disagreement among historians about the effectiveness of state economic policy. The view of Gerschenkron and von Laue that Witte's policies played a crucial role in the Russian industrial growth of the 1890s was rejected by Kahan, who argued that the burden of taxation and other state intervention restricted the scale of the market and of domestic investment; and that the costs of the transfer of the ruble (the Russian currency) onto the gold standard in the mid-1890s outweighed the benefits (Kahan 1967). Gregory also insists that state policies played a fairly minor role in industrialisation, which was primarily due to the growth of the Russian market economy and its integration in the world market. But unlike Kahan he holds that Russia's adoption of the gold standard was a prerequisite of her full participation in world trade and investment (Gregory 1994, pp. 54–80). Both these authors may underestimate the importance of the railways and defence in industrial expansion from 1890 to 1914 (Gatrell and Davies, 1990).

The debate among Soviet historians focused on different but related issues. V. I. Bovykin and others claimed that 'monopoly capitalism' (in Western terms, 'oligopolistic capitalism') had triumphed by the 1900s; the role of the state was secondary, and pre-capitalist structures should be seen as no more than survivals from the past. The alternative view, advocated by Tarnovsky, Volobuev and others, emphasised the co-existence of competing economic structures, including pre-capitalist structures, and stressed the multi-form and transitional character of the late Tsarist economy. This approach was first clearly formulated at the end of the 1960s. At that time the official Soviet view was that this was a 'departure from Marxism-Leninism'. Its protagonists were demoted and their writings were banned until history was liberated from official orthodoxy in the Gorbachev years.

These debates are directly relevant to the problem of interpreting both the collapse of Tsarism and the two revolutions of 1917: the liberal-democratic revolution of February/March; and the Communist revolution in October/November led by Lenin and the Bolshevik wing of the Social-Democratic Labour Party.[*] Bovykin supported the orthodox view that the maturity of Russian capitalism meant that the Bolshevik revolution was a classical socialist revolution led by the revolutionary industrial working class. In contrast, Volobuev and his associates stressed that the plurality of economic structures had given rise to social and economic problems which had revolutionised a variety of social classes; the relatively immature Russian working class could not have succeeded on its own.

A long-standing controversy within the Marxist school has concerned the role of foreign capital in Russian industrialisation. The pre-revolutionary economist P. V. Ol', whose statistical work on this subject has not yet been superseded, and N. Vanag, writing in the 1920s, claimed that Russian industry was overwhelmingly dominated by foreign capital. Their work was on the whole successfully challenged by Gindin, who insisted that the capital structure of Russian industry was a complex interleaving of

---

[*] The pre-revolutionary Julian calendar was thirteen days behind the Western Gregorian calendar. The Western calendar was introduced by the Bolshevik government on 1/14 February 1918.

Russian and foreign capital in different proportions in different industries. The Communist Party authorities eventually, with some reservations, supported Gindin. (Barber 1981, pp. 71–9.) Thus both the Soviet Communist Party and Gerschenkron stressed the independence of Russian capitalism in 1914. But they drew opposite conclusions from the same premise. The Communist Party stressed, in contrast to Trotsky, the leader of the 'Left Opposition' within the party in the 1920s, that Russian pre-revolutionary capital was strong enough to provide a basis for completing the construction of socialism in the Soviet Union without assistance from successful revolutions elsewhere. Gerschenkron, however, argued that, in view of the successful economic development undertaken by Russian capitalism, Soviet state-managed industrialisation was an unnecessary anachronism.

The debate has taken on new features in the 1980s and 1990s. Until the 1980s almost all Russian and many Western economists and economic historians assumed that large nations, while taking part in mutually beneficial foreign trade, would seek economic independence, and that this required them to develop a wide range of modern industries in which national capital and management were predominant. At the end of the twentieth century capitalism has become much more international, and most economists and historians now stress the benefits of foreign capital to pre-revolutionary Russian industrialisation rather than its disadvantages. Meanwhile much detailed investigation of the role of foreign capital in the pre-revolutionary economy remains to be undertaken: the work of Crisp and McKay is an important step in this direction (Crisp 1976; McKay 1970).

The various Marxist schools of thought all assume that contradictions within the economy and society were the fundamental causes of the breakdown of the old order and its overthrow in 1917. On this broad issue Western historians are divided. Many agree with Gerschenkron in stressing that a modern capitalist economy was successfully emerging in Tsarist Russia. As we have seen, there is no doubt that industry was developing rapidly. Paul Gregory has shown that the older view that agricultural output per head was declining in the decades before 1914 is mistaken (Gregory 1983). Some historians also argue that the Stolypin reforms led to even more rapid agricultural growth on the eve of the First World War, though it seems more likely that this was due to the favourable weather in these years (Wheatcroft 1990, pp. 83, 283).

Other historians reject the 'optimistic' view, and stress the continued backwardness and instability of the economy. They draw attention to the high regional concentration of industry: 60 per cent of the production of large-scale industry was located in the St Petersburg, Moscow and Ural regions; 20 per cent in Ukraine; and 10 per cent in the Transcaucasus (in the oil industry). Only 10 per cent was produced in the vast hinterland in which the majority of the population lived. Moreover, the industry of the Russian Empire lacked the most sophisticated forms of production (such as electrical goods and machinery, and capital equipment generally); and its research base was extremely narrow. In agriculture, the general rise in production concealed important symptoms of crisis. While grain production increased, the number of livestock per head declined. And grain output per head was declining in certain important regions – notably the Central Black-Earth region, where the countryside suffered from overpopulation and economic distress (Wheatcroft 1990, pp. 81–92).

Many historians stress that even if economic development was successful in its own terms, it carried with it profound social conflict. Leopold Haimson argues that the structure of Russian industry, with its large units, poor working conditions and oppressive discipline, made for social unrest and political radicalisation (Haimson 1988, p. 514). Teodor Shanin notes that the Russian economy produced 'crowded city slums' and 'the growing hopelessness of villagers in the most populous part of rural Russia'; the poor became 'reservoirs of poverty and class hatred ever arrayed against the manor houses and the "nice quarters"'(Shanin 1985, p. 200).

Other Western historians reject these economic and social explanations. They explain the collapse of Tsarism primarily in terms of the failure of its political system to adapt to the needs of a modernising society. On the reasons for this failure, opinions are divided. Some treat it as a profound structural problem (see Davies 1990, p. 23); others, including Hugh Seton-Watson, blame the narrowmindedness and obstinacy of the Tsar (Seton-Watson 1952, pp. 377–9).

So far we have only briefly mentioned the international context: the mounting crisis which culminated in the First World War. Some Western historians, including Gerschenkron, see the war as an unlucky accident, which interrupted the progressive course of Russian evolution towards capitalism and parliamentary democracy (Gerschenkron 1965, p. 141). In contrast, Soviet historians, following Lenin and other pre-revolutionary Marxists, saw the Russian economy as part of the international capitalist system. According to Lenin, 'imperialist war' between capitalist states was inevitable, and the half-developed Russian economy was bound to be shattered by the impact of war. Some influential Western historians, such as von Laue and Geyer, while rejecting Lenin's general view of the economic causes of war, argue that the drive to war was deeply rooted in the pre-war international system. Russia as a great power was inevitably involved in the drive to war. The Russian attempt to catch up the West placed enormous strains on the system, and these were greatly exacerbated when Russia confronted the economically more advanced Imperial Germany (von Laue 1966, pp. 36, 223; Geyer 1987, pp. 11, 345–6; Lieven 1983, pp. 153–4). On this view, the collapse of the Tsarist economy must be seen in the context of the profound contradictions within the European political order.

What is certain is that the First World War greatly exacerbated economic and social tensions (Gatrell 1994b). In the first eighteen months or so after July 1914, the economy appeared to prosper. The vast increase in armaments orders led to the rapid development not only of the armaments industries themselves, but also of the engineering industries serving armaments production, notably the infant machine-tool industry. Mobilisation removed large numbers of men from the countryside: by the end of 1917 over 15 million men had been recruited for the armed forces, most of them peasants. But the 1915 harvest was a good one; and the cancellation of grain exports (one-eighth of all grain production in 1913) meant that adequate grain was available to feed the population.

These apparently favourable trends were abruptly reversed in 1916. While armaments production continued to expand, the production of consumer goods declined by 12 per cent. In agriculture, the supply of agricultural machinery and implements fell to a mere 10 per cent of the pre-war level; and by 1916 the army had requisitioned 10 per cent of the horse population. The grain harvest of 1916 was poor.

But it was the inadequacy of the distribution and military planning system which was the main destabilising factor in the economy. By 1916, industrial labour was in short supply, only partly compensated by the extensive use of female labour and prisoners. And in the winter of 1916/17 food supplies to the towns fell drastically even though the urban population was increasing remorselessly. The decline in urban and military food supply triggered the mass discontent of the early months of 1917. At the same time the muddle and confusion in government reinforced the distrust and even contempt of the professional and business classes, largely excluded from political power, towards the Tsarist regime.

Most important of all, by the winter of 1916–17 the Russian Empire was creaking and cracking under the pressure of the armies of Germany and her allies, superior in the amount and quality of their weapons and the educational level of their soldiers. Like its predecessors, Nicholas II's Russia confronted economically more advanced powers with disastrous consequences. Peasants in uniform and middle classes joined the industrial working class in overturning the old regime. For the mass of the population food supplies and living conditions continued to deteriorate after the establishment of the Provisional Government by the February/March revolution, and fostered the continuing discontent which facilitated the victory of the Bolsheviks in the October/November revolution.

# 3

# War Communism, 1918–1920

In Tsarist Russia, as in the other combatant nations, the war greatly enhanced the role of the state. The state regulatory agencies were headed by a Special Council for Defence, which assigned military orders to industry. This was supported by more specific agencies such as the Metals Committee, which controlled the distribution of metals and fixed their prices. A Special Council for Food Supply attempted to set maximum prices; and the Provisional Government which came to power after the February revolution established a state grain monopoly. These instruments for controlling the economy varied considerably in their effectiveness and efficiency. But after October 1917 the Bolshevik or Soviet government was able to take over much of this planning apparatus and adapt it to its needs.

The Bolsheviks came to power with far-reaching objectives. Following Marx, they believed that the October revolution was the first victory of a world proletarian (working class) revolution which would transfer factories, the land and other means of production into social ownership by the state, local authorities or co-operatives. A planned economy directly controlled by the community would replace the market; money, the medium for market exchange, would cease to exist. In the first, 'socialist', phase of post-revolutionary development the social product would be distributed according to the quantity and quality of the work done by each individual. Later, the abundance of production achieved by the planned economy would enable the transition to the higher phase of 'communism', in which production would be distributed according to needs. Classes, the state and all national barriers would disappear.

Their immediate aims were far more modest. Marx anticipated that proletarian revolutions would take place in industrially advanced countries with a strong working class. But Russia was still largely an agrarian country. In the summer of 1917, some revolutionaries hoped for an immediate transformation of society in Russia. But Lenin and his immediate colleagues did not call for the establishment of a fully socialist economy in Russia, but for measures of state control and partial state ownership which would bring economic chaos to an end. Six months after the October revolution, in April 1918, Lenin called for a temporary halt to the rush towards full socialism, and consolidation of the gains achieved. The offensive against private capital must be temporarily halted; the modern achievements of capitalist organisation must be brought into industry; the currency must be stabilised (Lenin 1936–8, vii, pp. 313–35).

These proposals were soon superseded. By the summer of 1918 civil war and foreign intervention were well under way, and for two years the Soviet government was engaged in a desperate struggle for survival. In the autumn of 1919 its territory was no more extensive than that of sixteenth-century Muscovy. The rest of the former Russian Empire was controlled by various non-Communist governments. Some of these were managed by the minority nations of the former Empire, but the most important were the 'White' governments under the control of former Tsarist generals.

Within a few months of the outbreak of the Civil War, the system later described as 'War Communism' was firmly established. The core of War Communism was the compulsory acquisition of grain and other foodstuffs from the peasants by the state and its agencies, using armed force where necessary. The peasants received little or nothing in return. In theory, the central authorities allocated a quota to each region, and the quotas were in turn divided among the villages. In practice, requisitioning was quite arbitrary. The requisitioned foodstuffs were distributed to the army and to the urban population. In the towns an elaborate rationing system was introduced, graded according to the occupation of the consumer.

Industrial consumer goods were also brought under close central control, at least in principle. In industry, all firms of a substantial size, and many smaller firms, were nationalised. The central planning apparatus inherited from the Tsarist regime was greatly extended. Compulsory labour service and centralised direction of labour were also introduced, though more cautiously.

Inflation was rampant. With the near-collapse of the taxation system, the government sought to finance its activities through currency issue. By 1 January 1921, currency in circulation amounted to 1,168,597 million rubles as compared with 1,530 million rubles on 1 July 1914. But its purchasing power had declined to a mere 70 million pre-war rubles. Prices are estimated to have reached 16,800 times the 1914 level. (Davies 1958, pp. 9, 31.)

One further important feature of War Communism should be noted. The peasant economy remained more or less intact. During the agrarian revolution of 1917–18, which began spontaneously before the Bolsheviks took power, the land and property of the private estates were distributed among the peasants; and some equalisation took place between peasant households. All attempts by the government to encourage the collective or state ownership of former estates, and of the peasant economies, had almost no practical effect. State agencies had to deal with millions of peasant households.

The official economy was intended to embrace all economic activity, but in practice it was supplemented by illegal and semi-legal free markets. It is estimated that at the end of 1919 even workers' families in provincial capitals received less than half their grain, flour and potatoes from their official ration (Szamuely 1974, pp. 18–19). With the collapse of the currency, barter increasingly replaced money as a medium of exchange. The new regime could not have survived without this unofficial market economy.

Historians continue to debate the origins and function of War Communism. Some claim that it was primarily a result of the application of Marxist ideology, which was hostile to private property and the market; others stress, in the phrase of the British Marxist economist Maurice Dobb, that it was 'an improvisation in face of economic scarcity and military urgency in conditions of exhausting civil war' (Dobb 1948, p. 122). This question has been tackled in two ways. The first is by an examination of the emergence of each of the characteristic institutions of War Communism. The evidence seems to show that each major step was a response to emergency. The decree of 28 June 1918, which nationalised nearly all large enterprises, was prompted by fear that the German government was about to claim that important Russian firms should be exempted from nationalisation because they had been acquired by German citizens (Dobb 1928, pp. 59–60). The collapse of the currency was not primarily due to Bolshevik contempt for money. In 1918 and 1919 Lenin and his associates sought to stabilise the ruble, but were driven inexorably along the road of inflationary currency issue (Davies 1958, pp. 26–8). And the most crucial feature of the Civil War economy – the coercive collection of grain – was a response to the grave food shortages in the towns and the needs of the Red Army: 'we do it', one leading official declared, 'because there is not enough food' (Lih 1986, pp. 678–9).

Measures introduced in response to emergency were, however, often strongly influenced by Bolshevik ideology. For example, in requisitioning grain, the Bolsheviks exaggerated both the importance of the rich peasants (the *kulaks*) and the extent to which the poor peasants would be prepared to co-operate with the Bolsheviks against the *kulaks*. As Alec Nove put it, 'there was a process of *interaction* between circumstances and ideas' (Nove 1982, p. 48).

The second way to examine the question of improvisation versus ideology is to compare the rival experiences on the Soviet and 'White' territories. The White anti-Communist governments were all strongly biased in favour of private ownership and the market. Few detailed studies of the economic policies of these governments have yet been made. Available evidence indicates that on a number of crucial issues the White leaders were confronted by the same problems as the Bolsheviks and adopted similar solutions. Even in the grain-rich areas of southern Russia and Ukraine, following initial successes in feeding the population at relatively low prices, the governments of the Ukrainian nationalist Hetman Skoropadsky and the former Tsarist generals Denikin and Wrangel soon resorted to administrative measures and coercion to obtain grain. By the end of 1919 peasants were merely given paper receipts in exchange for requisitioned food. Wrangel invaded the Crimea in search of grain; and he even had to introduce a foreign trade monopoly in order to prevent grain being exported by private dealers. From mid-1919, the White governments in the south were also impelled to issue paper money in huge quantities, to the point of financial collapse. In the White as well as the Bolshevik areas, industrial production fell drastically. (Kenez 1977, pp. 94–102, 159, 162, 287–96.)

For the White governments, however, these measures of administrative control were purely a temporary expedient, to be cast aside in conditions of peace. Expediency had also driven the Bolsheviks towards a planned socialist moneyless economy far more rapidly than they had intended. But, in contrast to the Whites, the victorious Bolsheviks assumed throughout 1920 that the methods successful in war should be continued in time of peace. In February 1920, Lenin declared that the system of food requisitioning at fixed prices was a victory for socialism and should be used in economic reconstruction. The requisitioning system was continued after the harvest of 1920 and during the winter of 1920–1, when the Civil War had already come to an end. Moreover, in the winter of 1920–1, the Soviet government and its advisers sought to consolidate the moneyless economy, assuming that it would be a permanent feature of the peace-time economy. (Davies 1958, pp. 38–45; 1989a, pp. 1004–6.)

The 1917 revolutions and the Civil War brought about profound social changes. The nationalisation of all large-scale industry, banks and other property destroyed the wealth and authority of the former owners and removed the senior management of their enterprises. In the agrarian revolution of 1917–18 the peasants seized the land and other assets of the landowners and distributed them among themselves. The disappearance of the landowning class (about half a million people, including families) and the 'big' bourgeoisie (a further 125,000 or so) meant that the economy was effectively in new hands. Many landowners and businessmen were killed in the course of the Civil War; more emigrated. Recent research indicates that a mere 11 or 12 per cent of former landowners – mainly small landowners – remained in the countryside, often as peasants (Channon 1987, pp. 582–4).

On the eve of the First World War 136,000 specialists with higher education were active in the economy, and possibly a larger number of semi-professionals. Most professional people were hostile to the Bolshevik revolution, and it is often assumed that a very high proportion of them emigrated. No reliable count has yet been made, but this assumption seems not to be justified. In the case of medical doctors, for example, a high proportion remained in the USSR and continued to pursue their profession (Wheatcroft 1984, p. 23).

World war, revolutions and civil war resulted in a much greater social upheaval than is indicated by these figures. By the beginning of 1918, before the Civil War began, as a result of world war and revolution, 17.5 million persons remained unsettled, over 12 per cent of the total population. Many millions more were uprooted during the next few years. The large towns were denuded of population: between 1917 and 1920 the combined populations of Moscow and St Petersburg fell from 4.30 million to only 1.86 million. Over 2 million people emigrated. The disastrous famine of 1921–2, in the year following the Civil War, resulted in the flight of many more refugees in search of food. (Wheatcroft and Davies 1994b, pp. 60–2.)

Many people died prematurely. Some 3 million soldiers were killed, or died of wounds or disease. Some 13 million civilians died prematurely, mainly in the 1921–2 famine and in a series of epidemics which spread through Russia, above all the devastating influenza epidemic which affected most of Europe (Wheatcroft and Davies 1994b, pp. 62–3; Lorimer 1946, pp. 36–43). The population of the Soviet Union, at its lowest point in January 1923, was 6–9 million *fewer* than in January 1914 (within the same frontiers) (Wheatcroft and Davies 1994b, pp. 63–4). In 1914–22 the peoples of the Russian Empire/Soviet Union experienced privation, suffering and misery on an enormous scale.

# 4

# The New Economic Policy of the 1920s

The Soviet government abandoned its efforts to prolong War Communism into the time of peace; but only in response to a profound crisis. By 1920 War Communism had enabled the Soviet regime to establish itself over nearly the whole territory of the Russian Empire – with the exception of the Baltic states, Finland and Eastern Poland. But the economy was devastated. The output of large-scale industry had fallen to a mere 13 per cent of the 1913 level, iron and steel to a mere 4 per cent. Even small-scale artisan industry produced less than half its pre-war level. Grain output was only two-thirds of the 1909–13 average. Foreign trade had collapsed, amounting to less than 1 per cent of the 1913 turnover. (Gatrell 1994b, pp. 233, 231; Lewis 1994a, p. 201.)

In conditions of peace, the grain requisitioning policy and the other policies of War Communism were no longer viable. From the summer of 1920 peasant disturbances were widespread. From the beginning of 1921, the country plunged into a disastrous fuel, transport and food crisis, and unrest spread to the industrial workers. Against this tense background, in March 1921 the Xth Communist Party Congress decided to replace requisitioning by a food tax, which was fixed in advance at a lower level than the previous grain quotas. The peasants would retain any surplus. Their incentive to grow more food would thus be restored.

These decisions of March 1921 amounted to a quite limited reform. They assumed that peasants would dispose of their surpluses through local barter or by exchanging them for consumer goods provided by state agencies. Otherwise, War Communism, including the moneyless economy, would remain intact. This partial retreat proved to be unstable; Lenin later frankly admitted that 'the private market proved stronger than us'. Within a few months, what became known as the New Economic Policy (NEP) had emerged from the ruins of civil war.

The central feature of NEP was the right of individual peasants to sell their products freely, locally or nationally, to private traders, direct to other individuals, or to state agencies. Trade was resumed on a national scale, with most retail trade in private ownership. This was a retreat towards capitalism.

Nearly the whole of large-scale industry remained in state ownership. But artisan workshops and some small factories were rented or sold by the state to individual owners, and state industry was instructed to operate on principles of profit-and-loss accounting (*khozraschet*), and to adapt itself to the needs of the market. The wage system was restored, and enterprises were permitted to hire and fire workers in accordance with their needs. For the workers, all restrictions on changing jobs were removed; but they had to suffer the emergence of substantial urban unemployment.

The restoration of the market implied the restoration of the money economy. Following a period of dramatic further inflation, the currency was gradually stabilised. Drastic reductions were made in every kind of state expenditure, and the taxation system was restored. The process culminated in the currency reform of March 1924. Simultaneously the tax in kind on peasant households gave way to a tax in money.

NEP thus resulted in a mixed monetary economy, in which state industry traded with individual peasant agriculture through a market which was partly in state hands, partly in private hands. The market operated within definite constraints. On the one hand, the state refrained from the use of coercion against the peasants: the state was required to offer prices to the peasants which they were prepared to accept voluntarily. On the other hand, firm limits were imposed on the development of capitalism. All major banking institutions as well as large-scale industry remained in state hands. Stringent conditions were imposed on foreign firms seeking to invest in Soviet industry. The state maintained its monopoly of foreign trade, so that all imports required a licence, and the earnings from all exports were managed by the state. And the market economy operated within a strict political framework.

While much freedom of discussion was permitted, during 1921–2 the one-party Communist dictatorship was consolidated, discipline within the party was tightened up, and an elaborate system of preliminary censorship was established. This political dictatorship continued for nearly seventy years.

After the initial setback of the disastrous famine of 1921–2, the pace of recovery was extremely rapid. By 1927 or 1928 both agricultural and industrial production exceeded their pre-war levels. The extent of the recovery is disputed. According to the lowest Western estimate, by Paul Gregory, in 1928 Soviet net national income (gross national income less depreciation) had reached only 93 per cent of the 1913 level; according to the official Soviet estimate, it reached 119 per cent of the 1913 level (Gregory 1990, p. 337). Our own revised estimate of 111 per cent lies between these two limits: it implies that national income per head of population had just recovered to the pre-war level (these estimates are discussed in Harrison 1994a, pp. 42, 333 n.10).

Technically, this was largely the same economy as before the revolution. In the urban economy, recovery depended on bringing back into use the pre-1917 factories, mines, shops and offices, reassembled, patched up and put to work. The oil industry, where substantial new investment took place in 1923–7, was a rare exception (Gatrell and Davies 1990, p. 132). In agriculture in the mid-1920s peasant cultivation – responsible for 90 per cent of the sown area in 1914 – continued largely by traditional methods.

But the revolution and its aftermath brought about profound changes in social relations which had a considerable impact on the way the economy was run. The Soviet Union in the mid-1920s was a more equal society than the Russian Empire in 1914. The revolution had flattened the top and extended the sides of the steep pre-revolutionary pyramid. In trade and industry, in spite of the encouragement given to small-scale private industry in the early years of NEP, private entrepreneurs were far smaller in number, and far less wealthy per head, than before the revolution. Industrial workers were now employed in state rather than private industry. It is often assumed that the pre-revolutionary working class had been dissipated and diluted by the upheavals of 1914–20. But many and perhaps most of those recruited in 1922–5 had worked in industry before 1917. This was largely a second-generation working class, which retained contacts with the villages, but did not hold land there (Barber 1978).

The industrial workers were the heroes of the revolution and its main beneficiaries. The introduction of the eight-hour day reduced the average working day from 9.9 hours in 1913 to 7.8 in 1928. The authority of the engineer and the foreman over the worker was considerably diminished as compared with pre-revolutionary times. Within the working class, the differentiation in earnings between skilled and unskilled was substantially narrower than in 1914. Women workers were more numerous than in 1914, and benefited from the legislation which introduced equal pay for equal work. But dark clouds overshadowed these triumphs. Ever since 1917 the Communist Party in power had circumscribed and destroyed any political opposition which appealed to the working class interest. By the mid-1920s the workers had effectively lost their hard-won right to strike (though illegal strikes still occurred on a small scale).

In the countryside, as well as the towns, greater equality prevailed. The land and property of the landowners had been distributed among the peasants. Within the village, the *kulaks* (richer peasants) were relatively less wealthy than before the revolution, and many formerly landless peasants had acquired land. The rural economy had undergone what was generally known as 'middle-peasantisation' (*oserednyachenie*) (Danilov 1988, pp. 205–58; Davies 1980, pp. 4–31).

The social upheaval brought with it fundamental changes in the process of capital accumulation, with quite different results in the industrial and the agricultural sectors. In industry, the railways and most internal trade, the dearth of private savings meant that capital accumulation overwhelmingly depended on the state. The private and artisan sectors were responsible for a mere 4 per cent of industrial investment in the economic year 1926/7 (Davies 1989b, p. 490). In contrast, in agriculture it was the 25 million individual peasant households which undertook their own investment in the form of purchasing machinery and implements, largely from the state, breeding livestock and building dwellings and farm buildings. Only 5 per cent of agricultural investment took place in the socialised sector in 1926/7 (Davies 1989b, p. 490).

How far did the industrial sector indirectly or directly draw its resources from agriculture? This has proved to be a very difficult question to answer. Harrison concludes that direct and indirect taxation of the peasants was lower in 1928 than in 1913; while the terms of trade for agriculture were much less favourable, the low level of urban–rural trade limited the transfer of resources from agriculture to industry. On balance, according to Harrison, there was 'a substantial reduction in the peasant contribution to industrial capital formation' (Harrison 1990a).

The relation between agriculture and industry was the central preoccupation of the authorities. The towns depended on the peasantry for their food, and the needs of the town would necessarily grow with the expansion of industry. However, although agricultural production had recovered to the pre-war level, agricultural marketings throughout the 1920s were substantially lower than before the war. The share of agricultural output leaving the village had fallen from 22–25 per cent of the total in 1913 to 16–17 per cent in the mid-1920s. It seems reasonably certain that grain marketing had fallen to little more than half the pre-war level, though this has been doubted by some historians. (Harrison 1990a, pp. 110–11, 285; Karcz 1966/7; Davies 1969/70; Karcz 1970/1.)

One important consequence of the decline was that foreign trade utterly failed to recover to the pre-war level. In the economic year 1926/7 exports amounted to only 33 per cent and imports to only 38 per cent of the 1913 level. This decline, entirely due to the fall in agricultural exports, was itself primarily a consequence of the decline in agricultural marketings, particularly of grain, the main pre-revolutionary export. Even in the best year of NEP, grain exports amounted to only one-quarter of the 1913 level (Davies 1990, pp. 324–5, 331).

Why did agricultural marketings decline? One significant factor, strongly emphasised by Soviet historians, was the change in the socio-economic structure of the countryside. The abolition of the market-oriented landowners' estates, and the marked decline in socio-economic differentiation among the peasantry following the agrarian revolution of 1917–18, may both have had a negative effect on marketings (Harrison 1990a, pp. 112–13, 361 n. 20). The increase in the number of peasant households from 20 million

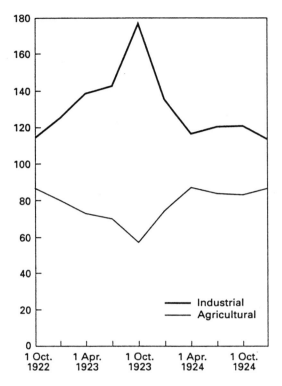

Figure 1. Agricultural and industrial prices, 1922–5, illustrating the 'scissors crisis' of 1923. Graphs show wholesale price indices of Gosplan (1913=100).

to 25 million, and the consequent decline in the size of each household, may also have played its part. A second important factor was the reduced level of peasant taxation and the elimination of land rents. Direct taxation and land rents taken together fell from about 10 per cent to about 5 per cent of farm incomes between 1913 and 1926/7 (Harrison 1990a, pp. 113, 287, 361 n. 22).

Thirdly, terms of trade for agricultural produce generally deteriorated in comparison with 1913, and this probably discouraged peasants from marketing their output. The ratio of the retail prices of manufactured goods to the prices received by the peasants for their produce was less favourable to the peasants than before the war. This problem first emerged in the economic crisis of 1923, known as the 'scissors crisis': Trotsky, in a striking image, compared the graph showing these two price levels to the open blades of a pair of scissors (see figure 1). In the 1920s, Soviet economists of all schools of thought believed that the 'scissors' would discourage the peasants from selling their produce, and encourage them to retain it for their own consumption. More recently, the American economist James Millar has argued that this is not true, because peasant demand for manufactured goods was price-inelastic. In consequence, when the terms of trade deteriorated, peasants were forced to sell *more* products in order to obtain essential manufactured goods (Millar 1974; Millar and Nove 1976). Strenuous attempts to check this hypothesis have been unsuccessful (Harrison 1990a, pp. 113–14, 361 nn. 25–7). It is chastening to reflect that we are perhaps being unreasonable to expect Soviet politicians to have adopted sensible agricultural price policies in the 1920s, when we are unable over seventy years later to agree about even the general direction in which prices should have moved.

Whatever may be the truth about terms of trade as a whole, it is certain that the particularly low level of marketings in the case of grain was due to the low price of grain relative to other agricultural products. The authorities were confronted with a delicate balance. If they increased the relative level of grain prices, peasants tended to switch resources away from industrial crops essential as raw materials for industry (raw sugar, flax, cotton, etc., depending on the agricultural region). This happened in the summer of 1925. On the other hand, if they reduced grain prices too far, as they did after the 1926 harvest, the peasants withheld grain and reduced their grain sowings. A further problem was that meat and dairy products, unlike grain, were mainly sold on the private market rather than to the state. Hence these prices could not be controlled without a considerable increase in direct state management.

Agricultural marketings were unstable as well as insufficient. Only two harvests in the 1920s – those of 1922 and 1926 – escaped serious economic difficulties resulting from inadequate marketings. These fluctuations were partly due to Russian climatic conditions which resulted in great annual variation in the harvest.

But they were also a result of failures in policy. Maintenance of equilibrium on the market between a relatively small number of state enterprises and 25 million individual peasant households proved to be a delicate task – and the political leaders were unable or unwilling to adjust their policies flexibly to changing market conditions. But a more fundamental dilemma lurked behind the successive crises. On the one hand, the Soviet authorities were constantly preoccupied with the danger that supplies of food to the towns and the army and of agricultural raw materials to industry would be inadequate. On the other hand, the persistent efforts of the same authorities to increase the share of resources available to industry constantly threatened the economic basis of the relationship between the regime and the peasantry.

The urgent necessity of developing industry was accepted by nearly all shades of opinion within the Communist Party and by most of their economic advisers. Marx had held that the prerequisite for the establishment of a socialist society was the existence of a modern industrial economy employing a class-conscious industrial working class. But Communist power had been established in a peasant country. The Soviet leaders concluded that the Communist political superstructure must itself organise and force through the development of modern industry, performing the role undertaken by the bourgeoisie in Western Europe and the United States. Modernisation must be imposed from above.

Doctrinal arguments were supported by practical considerations. The Soviet Union had emerged less than a decade earlier from a civil war in which foreign capitalist powers had sought to destroy the Communist regime. This seemed to demonstrate the necessity for a broadly based industry which would provide the basis for defence against a hostile world – and perhaps for the support of foreign revolutionary movements. But, in an international perspective, the restored economy of 1928 was in a less favourable position than the Russian Empire of 1913. The other Great Powers had suffered less from the war and its aftermath than Soviet Russia. By 1928, the industrialised capitalist economies were at the peak of the inter-war trade cycle. The gap in production per head of population between Soviet and Western European industry was as wide as ever, and the gap with the

United States had widened. Even more significantly, as a result of technological advances in the West, particularly in Germany and the United States, the technological gap between Russia and the other Great Powers was considerably greater than in 1913 (Gatrell and Davies 1990, pp. 154–7; Cooper and Lewis 1990, pp. 189–211).

Belief in the need to develop industry was reinforced by an unexpected and unwelcome feature of NEP: the growth of mass unemployment. The number of unemployed people increased continuously throughout the twenties. Even on a narrow definition, unemployment amounted to 9 per cent of the employed population at the end of 1926 (the employed population excludes peasants, artisans and others working on their own account). This was certainly a much higher number than on the eve of the war. In contrast to the situation in Western Europe and the United States at the time, the prime cause of unemployment was not economic depression – the number of employed persons increased rapidly in the 1920s. The main factor was the huge scale of rural migration into the towns, a familiar problem in Third World countries. Unemployment was a constant reproach to the authorities, and seemed to confront them with an insoluble dilemma. To finance the growth of industry, they sought to increase productivity and rationalise administration, but this necessarily restricted employment possibilities. The pace of industrialisation feasible within the framework of the market economy of NEP might alleviate unemployment, but it could not eliminate it.

Matters came to a head with the grain crisis of 1927–8. In the months October–December 1927, peasants sold only half as much grain to the official grain collection agencies as in the same period in 1926. With this amount of grain the towns and the army could not be fed.

Historians differ among themselves about the reasons for the grain crisis. Traditionally, Soviet historians, reflecting the explanations offered by Stalin at the time, attributed the failure to supply grain to the changed post-revolutionary socio-economic structure of agriculture, combined with sabotage by the *kulaks*. In contrast, some Western political historians treat the grain shortages as having been created artificially by Stalin, and used by him as a pretext to crack down on the peasants (Conquest 1986, pp. 87–

93). Other Western historians have stressed the effect on the relationship between the towns and the countryside of the substantial increase in industrial investment during the economic year 1926/7. The increase was particularly rapid in the capital goods industries, which did not provide an immediate return in the form of consumer goods (Carr and Davies 1969, pp. 291–2, 773–5). Other historians place more emphasis on the erroneous price policies, which themselves were rooted in Bolshevik attitudes to the market (Nove 1982, pp. 138–42). A striking example in favour of this view is provided by the reduction of industrial retail prices in the spring of 1927. This greatly exacerbated the goods shortage in the countryside, and thus contributed to the peasants' reluctance to sell their grain (Davies 1980, pp. 39–40). My own view is that both the expansion of the resources devoted to industry and erroneous price policies were major causes of the crisis.

The grain crisis illustrated the general dilemma of NEP. NEP had proved successful in bringing about the revival of the economy to the pre-war level. But could it provide an effective framework for the industrialisation of the Soviet Union, for achieving the goal accepted by all wings of the Communist Party – to catch up and overtake the advanced capitalist countries?

This was the central issue in the Soviet debates on general economic strategy which took place in the 1920s. These debates, mainly conducted within the framework of Marxist economics, preceded by twenty or thirty years the discussions of the 'economics of underdevelopment' in the West. Like Witte in the 1890s, the participants showed a remarkable grasp of what many economists now consider to be the essential issues in the process of industrialisation in peasant economies. The Soviet debates were first examined by Dobb in 1928; interest in them revived in the 1960s with the publication of the thorough surveys by Erlich and Spulber; an account based on personal experience was published by Jasny (Dobb 1928; Erlich 1960; Spulber 1964; Jasny 1972).

A number of rival strategies were proposed. Sokolnikov, who was People's Commissar of Finance in 1924 and 1925, did not share the common assumption that industry must be developed immediately. He argued that the return on investment in agriculture was, in the circumstances of the 1920s, much greater than the return on industry. Hence industrialisation could be best achieved by investing in agriculture for the time being, and exporting grain to pay for imports of cheap machinery.

Sokolnikov's view of the importance of agriculture was supported by strong groups of agrarian economists, whose views and analysis received a great deal of publicity in the mid-1920s. While Sokolnikov saw the development of agriculture as the best way forward to industrial development, most of the agrarian economists were primarily concerned with the development of agriculture as such – and particularly of peasant family economies. Most prominent was the internationally renowned Nikolai Kondratiev, of 'long cycles' fame. Kondratiev, like Stolypin before the revolution, stressed the need for the peasant economies to adapt to the market and become efficient, even if this involved increased socio-economic differentiation among the peasants. In contrast, Chayanov strongly favoured co-operation between agricultural households on a voluntary basis. (For Kondratiev, see Barnett 1995; for Chayanov, see Solomon 1977.)

Most other economists shared Bolshevik enthusiasm for industrialisation, but held widely varying views about how to achieve it. Bazarov, who worked for the State Planning Commission, sought what Erlich described as 'relaxation possibilities' by advocating investment in those industries which would serve a mass market (e.g. textiles and agricultural implements) and hence would produce at low costs.

In contrast, Preobrazhensky, the principal economist in the Left Opposition headed by Trotsky, argued that the USSR must pass through a stage of 'primary socialist accumulation' analogous to the 'primary accumulation' postulated by Marx in his analysis of capitalism. Part of the product or incomes of the peasant economies should be exploited or 'alienated' by the state, through taxation or price policy, and transferred to industrial investment.

The prevailing opinion among advisers to the Soviet government in the mid-1920s, in contrast to both Sokolnikov and Preobrazhensky, was that sufficient savings for industrialisation could be found within industry, or within the state sector of the economy as a whole, by a rationalisation policy which would result in falling costs and increased profits. These savings would be achieved primarily by increasing labour productivity more rapidly than money wages.

Until the end of 1927 it was common ground among the different groups of politicians and schools of thought that the market economy of the 1920s would remain intact, and that the peasant would not be coerced. This principle was advocated most forcefully by the leading Communist intellectual Bukharin; but at this time it was also shared by Stalin, and even by Trotsky, Preobrazhensky and the Left Opposition. In view of later developments it is ironic that in 1924–7 Stalin and Bukharin strongly criticised the Left Opposition for its alleged advocacy of policies of 'super-industrialisation' which would damage the support of the peasantry for the Communist regime. (See Cohen 1974, pp. 270–336.)

The Stalin–Bukharin alliance broke up in face of the grain crisis of 1927–8. By this time Stalin was already the dominant figure in Soviet politics, and the reaction of Stalin and his associates to the crisis was firm and unhesitating. The so-called 'emergency measures' adopted by the Politburo in the winter of 1927–8 were strikingly different from the methods by which a similar crisis had been handled in 1925, only two years earlier. In the summer and autumn of 1925, the first substantial capital construction since the revolution had resulted in a considerable increase in demand. Serious shortages of goods resulted; and the peasants, confronted by empty shelves, reduced their sales of grain. The state reacted by increasing the price of grain and reducing the resources available to industry, so as to restore equilibrium on the market. (Carr 1958, pp. 290–7, 305–8; Davies 1980, p. 30.) At the end of 1927, however, the authorities kept the price of grain stable and pressed ahead with industrialisation. The consequent emergency measures at the beginning of 1928 involved the extensive use of compulsion to obtain grain. As in the Civil War, the authorities also unsuccessfully endeavoured to win the support of the mass of the peasants against the *kulaks*. While some peasants resented the economic and social power of the better-off, most correctly concluded that the grain policies of the state were against the economic interests of the majority of peasant households.

This was the beginning of the end of NEP. In recent work by historians and economists, both in the former Soviet Union and in the West, the collapse of NEP and its replacement by the Stalinist strategy of forced industrialisation have been central interests. In examining the strategy of Soviet industrialisation, historians echo, repeat and enlarge upon these debates of the 1920s, and dress themselves in the clothes of the rival schools, just as nineteenth-century historians of the French Revolution appeared as Girondins, Jacobins, Bonapartists or Monarchists. But, like the French historians, they are also able to stand outside and above these debates. Nearly all historians now agree that the differences in strategy between Trotsky and Bukharin were minor compared with their common rejection of the strategy adopted by Stalin.

In the assessment of NEP in these recent debates at least four approaches may be distinguished. First, many economists hold that NEP restricted market forces too greatly, even in the years of the mid-1920s when the greatest freedom was allowed to the private sector. Central price controls, in operation since 1923, and detailed state management of investment meant that the efficient allocation of resources was impossible. Alexander Gerschenkron even argued that the Bolshevik revolution was a fundamentally reactionary event, which reversed the rise of democratic capitalism. According to Gerschenkron, by the mid-1920s 'the conditions for economic growth would seem to have been rather unfavourable' (Gerschenkron 1965, pp. 144–60). This view is broadly shared by the many present-day Russian economists who have insisted that post-Gorbachev Russia must be transformed into a capitalist country, and that no 'Third Way' between capitalism and centralised state socialism is possible. According to Grigorii Khanin, for example, the last chance for a successful development of the Russian economy 'was lost at the beginning of the 1920s, and even then it was small'.

A second group of historians, among whom the late E. H. Carr is the most prominent, concurs that the economy of NEP was inherently unstable, if not a blind alley. But Carr's standpoint was radically different. He believed that the world economy is evolving from private capitalism to forms of state planning, and that in this context there was 'a latent incompatibility between the principles of the New Economic Policy and the principles of planning' (Carr 1978, p. 278). This general viewpoint, applied to the specific Soviet conditions of the 1920s, is also advocated by some modern

Russian historians. Thus M. M. Gorinov assesses the potential of NEP very pessimistically, concluding that 'the threat of technical backwardness, the permanent danger of war, and the instability of the market cast very grave doubt on the effectiveness of this variant'.

A third group, very influential in recent Western discussions, argued that NEP was compatible with successful long-term economic development. Stephen Cohen, the biographer of Bukharin, and Robert Tucker, the biographer of Stalin, strongly sympathise with the viewpoint of Bukharin, chief figure in the 'Right Wing' opposition to Stalin in 1928–9, who insisted that the only acceptable solution to the grain crisis was to restore equilibrium on the market and fit industrialisation into the NEP framework (Cohen 1974, ch. 9; Tucker 1974, ch. 12). And James Millar, logically applying his hypothesis that peasants would sell more of their production if its relative price was reduced, argued that NEP was compatible with at least as rapid a rate of industrialisation as that actually achieved (Millar 1974, p. 766).

The American economist Holland Hunter and his associates broadly belong to the same school of thought. Using a series of computer models to project alternative policy variants, they assume an NEP-type framework, without such taut planning and without the collectivisation of agriculture, and seek to demonstrate that with these alternative policies much better results could have been achieved. However, unlike Millar, Hunter assumes that, together with 'punitive taxation', it was also 'low prices for farm products in 1928 [which] made peasants less willing to produce and deliver output to the state' (Hunter and Szyrmer 1992, p. 90).

The view that NEP provided a viable system of successful industrialisation dominated Soviet popular publications about the Soviet past in 1988, and was the subject of several serious historical studies (described in Davies 1989c, chs. 3, 4).

The fourth group of historians, including myself, takes an intermediate position between the second and third group. We argue that the economy of the mid-1920s had not yet reached an impasse. In the economic year 1926/7, net investment in the economy as a whole had probably reached 90 per cent of the 1913 level, and net industrial investment was higher than in 1913 (Gatrell and Davies 1990, pp. 127–8). This success for planned industrialisation was accomplished before the grain crisis, and within the framework of NEP. In our opinion, given sensible price policies, a moderate rate of expansion of both industry and agriculture could have continued. On the other hand, we do not believe that NEP was capable of sustaining much higher rates of industrialisation than those achieved on the eve of the First World War.

On this view, judgement about the long-term economic viability of NEP depends on a political assessment of how far it was essential for the Soviet Union to establish powerful capital goods and armaments industries in the space of a few years.

# 5

# Measuring Soviet economic growth

The rapid pace of social and economic change in the crucial decades from 1928 to 1965 is inherently difficult to capture in the statistics. At the time of the 1926 population census, the urban population amounted to only 16 per cent of the total; by the time of the 1939 census, the proportion had doubled, to 33 per cent. The first census after the Second World War, in 1959, recorded that the urban population had reached 48 per cent of the total; and for 1965 it was estimated at 53 per cent. In the period 1928–65 the number of people employed in industry, construction and transport increased nearly sixfold, from 6,554,000 to 38,932,000. By 1965, according to a careful Western estimate, industrial production was fourteen times as great as in 1928; and even the sceptical Russian economist Khanin estimated that it was eleven times as great (see table 10, p. 82; for Khanin's estimate see Harrison 1993, p. 147). Such a rate of social change and industrial expansion, achieved in spite of the destruction of industrial capacity brought about by the German invasion of 1941–5, was without precedent at that time (though it has since been equalled or exceeded by several Asian countries).

During this period the composition of industrial production changed even more radically. In 1928, the machine-building industry was unsophisticated and fairly small. As early as the mid-1930s, it was the most important single industry, and its output included complex machine-tools, iron and steel-making equipment, tanks and many other products which it had not manufactured at all in 1928 (armaments in Soviet statistics were treated as part of machine-building). By the second half of the 1930s much machinery and armaments was mass-produced; far more invest-

Table 1 *Gross national product, 1928 and 1937*

|  | 1928 | 1937 | Index of GNP for 1937 (1928=100) |
|---|---|---|---|
|  | (billion rubles) | | |
| In 1928 prices | 30.0 | 81.3 | 271 |
| In 1937 prices | 132.9 | 215.6 | 162 |

*Source:* Bergson 1961, pp. 128, 153.

ment had been devoted to these industries than to food and consumer goods. Consequently, the cost of producing machinery and arms fell relative to that for food and consumer goods.

These developments strongly influenced the alternative indices of industrial production. When Soviet industrial production is valued in constant prices of 1928, the growth rate is dominated by high-cost machinery, and is exceptionally rapid. When prices of a later year (1937, 1940 or 1955) are used, the index is dominated by the high-priced and more slowly growing food and consumer goods, and the rate of growth appears to be slower. Industrial production and GNP (gross national product) increase much more rapidly when measured in 1928 prices than when measured in the prices of the final year of the particular index (end-year prices). Table 1 shows the startling results which were obtained by the American economist Bergson, using the same underlying data but different prices.

This phenomenon is known, after its discoverer, as 'the Gerschenkron effect' (we have already met the fertile mind of Alexander Gerschenkron in chapter 2 with his hypothesis on growth in conditions of economic backwardness). It is not unique to the Soviet Union. It is also observed, for example, in United States output statistics for the decades before the First World War – though over a longer time-span, as United States' industrial production increased more slowly.

The proportions of GNP devoted to different uses also differ according to the prices used. Investment and defence expenditure are both a much higher proportion of the total when GNP is measured in 1928 prices rather than in 1937 prices. This is because machinery, equipment, etc. are major elements in both investment and defence expenditure, and, as we have seen, their

Table 2 *Gross national product by end-use, 1928 and 1937*

| | (Percentages) | | | |
| | In 1928 prices | | In 1937 prices | |
| | 1928 | 1937 | 1928 | 1937 |
|---|---|---|---|---|
| Household consumption | 64.7 | 32.5 | 79.5 | 52.5 |
| Communal services | 5.1 | 7.7 | 4.6 | 10.5 |
| Government administration | 2.7 | 2.5 | 2.1 | 3.2 |
| Defence | 2.5 | 13.0 | 1.3 | 7.9 |
| Gross investment | 25.0 | 44.3 | 12.5 | 25.9 |
| Total | 100.0 | 100.0 | 100.0 | 100.0 |

*Source:* As for table 1.

costs and prices relative to those of other goods were much higher in 1928 than in 1937. This is again shown in Bergson's estimates (table 2).

Thus both the rate of Soviet growth and its structure change fundamentally with the change in the basis of measurement. Neither 1928 prices nor 1937 prices can be considered 'the more correct'. The first looks at development from the vantage-point of 1928; the second from the vantage-point of 1937. It should be noted, however, that measurement of Soviet production in international prices such as in US dollars gives a result closer to that in 1937 prices, because Soviet 1937 prices were closer to world prices than Soviet 1928 prices.

In addition to this *index number* effect, the Soviet rate of growth was also exaggerated because of *hidden inflation* in the prices used. In preparing their index, the authorities often included new products not in the prices of the initial year, but in the prices of the year in which they were introduced. As the general level of prices rose quite sharply in the early 1930s, this practice meant that production of later years was overvalued.

It has often been assumed that the inclusion of new products at artificially high prices particularly exaggerated the increase in machinery production. But the fall in cost of production of items such as tractors and lorries tended to *reduce* the prices of later years in respect of these items. It is the Soviet index for foodstuffs and consumer goods which is greatly exaggerated (Davies, Harrison and Wheatcroft 1994, p. 140). During the Second World

Table 3 *Index of munitions output, 1940–4*

|  | (1940 = 100) | | | |
|  | 1941 | 1942 | 1943 | 1944 |
| --- | --- | --- | --- | --- |
| Soviet official index | 140 | 186 | 224 | 251 |
| Harrison index | 148 | 307 | 365 | 389 |

*Sources:* Harrison 1994b, p. 241; Harrison 1996, pp. 190–1.

War, the increased scale of armaments production meant that the prices of weapons fell sharply, but the official index did not take this into account. Harrison's recalculation of the index of munitions output shows a Gerschenkron effect in reverse (table 3). But this is an exception to the normal tendency of the official index to exaggerate considerably the rate of growth.

At worst, Soviet statistics were deliberately falsified. The most famous case is that of the harvest of grain and other crops. From 1933 onwards, grain output was measured – without any public statement that a change had been made – in terms of 'biological' yield. This was the maximum possible yield of the crop standing in the field at the time of maximum ripeness, without any allowance for losses in harvesting and transport. The official statistics showed that grain output in 1939 amounted to 106.5 million tonnes, 58 per cent above the average harvest on the eve of the First World War; Wheatcroft's revision shows a harvest of 73 million tonnes, an increase of only 7 per cent, and he suspects that even this figure may be too high (Davies, Harrison and Wheatcroft 1994, pp. 286–7).

As a result of these various biases and distortions, the official index showed a far greater rate of growth of GNP than the recalculations by Western economists.

With the advent of *glasnost'* in the Soviet Union, a number of Russian economists and journalists have proposed far greater downward revisions than the Western estimates. Thus Grigorii Khanin claimed that Soviet GNP increased by only 50 per cent between 1928 and 1941. However, the Russian economists have not made available enough information about their methods of calculation to enable their results to be checked. For the period from the 1930s to the 1950s, the Bergson and

Table 4 *Gross national product, 1928–60*

| | 1937 | 1940 | (1928 = 100) 1950 | 1955 | 1960 | 1965 |
|---|---|---|---|---|---|---|
| Official Soviet index | 386 | 513 | 843 | 1442 | 2232 | 3063 |
| Bergson: 1928 prices at factor cost | 271 | – | – | – | – | – |
| Bergson: 1937 prices at factor cost | 162 | 197 | 243 | 350 | – | – |
| Moorsteen and Powell: 1937 prices | 172 | 203 | 246 | 357 | 507 | – |
| CIA: 1982 prices at factor cost | – | – | – | 313 | 408 | 517 |

*Note*: Gross national product is the final value of all goods and services, without any deduction for depreciation. Factor cost is defined as market prices less net indirect taxes.
*Sources*: Clarke 1972, p. 6; Bergson 1961, pp. 128, 153; Moorsteen and Powell 1966, pp. 361–2; *Measures* 1990, pp. 54–5. The CIA figures have been chained to the Moorsteen–Powell figure for 1960.

Moorsteen–Powell estimates certainly remain the most reliable (table 4).

Once all these corrections are made, the annual rate of growth of GNP remains quite impressive by international standards: omitting the war years, it amounted to 5–6 per cent in the period 1928–40 (10 per cent if measured in 1928 prices) and between 5 and 7.5 per cent in the 1950s. Simon Kuznets, comparing these rates with those in a variety of countries in the nineteenth and twentieth centuries, concluded that 'the USSR stands out with a high rate of growth of total and per capita product' (Bergson and Kuznets 1963, p. 342).

# 6
# Soviet economic development, 1928–1965

Soviet economic growth in these years falls into four distinct periods: (1) the pre-war industrialisation drive, 1928–41; (2) the Second World War, 1941–5; (3) post-war recovery, 1946–50; (4) post-war expansion, 1950–65.

## The pre-war industrialisation drive, 1928–1941

The figures for GNP as a whole do not reveal the most striking feature of Soviet economic development: the extraordinarily rapid development of industry, and particularly of capital goods, in contrast to the poor performance of agriculture. As table 10 (p. 82) shows, according to a Western estimate industrial output trebled between 1928 and 1940, increasing by nearly 10 per cent a year. These developments led industry to be concentrated into much larger units than in the Tsarist period. While one-third of industrial production came from small-scale industry in 1913, by 1937 the proportion had fallen to only 6 per cent (Kaufman 1962, p. 58).

The expansion of capital goods industries and the advance of their technology were very uneven. The pressure for more output in conditions in which unskilled labour was relatively abundant resulted in the employment of much more labour per unit of output, particularly in auxiliary processes, than in the major Western industrial countries. This was a kind of dual technology, and was well described as 'a labour-intensive variant of capital-intensive technology'.

How far were these developments dependent on foreign technical know-how and the import of foreign technology? During the early 1930s many foreign firms and individuals provided technical assistance to the major capital projects; and several thousand engineers and industrial workers were employed in design institutes, on capital projects and in factories. And strict controls over foreign trade enabled imports to be concentrated on machinery and equipment for the key industries. The relative importance of foreign machinery is difficult to assess. An American economist estimated the share of imports in the total value of new machinery installed in the economic year 1929/30 at 16 per cent. In contrast the Russian economist Khanin puts the proportion at 25 per cent for the whole period 1928–40, and as high as 80 per cent during the first five-year plan (1928–32); Khanin's results are in turn rejected by a British economic historian, who argues that they are based on an underestimation of the growth rate of domestic machinery production (Lewis 1994a, pp. 206–15). After 1932 the role of foreign imports and know-how declined considerably; the low level of foreign trade in the later 1930s no doubt delayed further technological advance in the Soviet Union.

The 1930s saw the vast expansion of the capital goods industries. Fuel and energy were supplied by the rapid expansion of the Donbass coal industry and the Baku and Grozny oil-fields, and by the construction of a vast network of electric power stations, including the famous dam and hydro-electric plant on the river Dnieper. A modern iron and steel industry was developed both in Ukraine and on the greenfield site at Magnitogorsk in the Urals (Kotkin 1995). On this basis new engineering industries were established: iron and steel-making equipment at Sverdlovsk (Ekaterinburg) in the Urals and Zaporozh'e in Ukraine; large tractor and agricultural machinery factories at Stalingrad (Volgograd), Khar'kov, Rostov and elsewhere; and an impressive range of machine-tool factories. Many of these branches of engineering were established almost from scratch in the 1930s. On this basis the USSR developed a modern armaments industry producing tanks and military aircraft as well as the artillery and warships for which pre-revolutionary Russia was already renowned. (See Davies, Harrison and Wheatcroft 1994, pp. 131–57.)

In the course of these developments substantial changes took place in the location of industry. Before 1930 industry was primarily situated in north-west and central European Russia and in Ukraine. In the 1930s the Soviet authorities sought to construct a major part of new industry in the Urals and Siberia, and in economically poorly developed Central Asia. In these areas there were vast mineral resources, which were unused and largely unexplored. Soviet social policy imperatively required development of the 'colonial' areas of Central Asia. And above all defence considerations required the construction of capital goods and armaments industries far from the frontier.

In the 1930s the industrial output of the Urals and Trans-Urals regions increased from 11 or 12 per cent of the total in 1928 to over 16 per cent in 1940. But developing these new areas was expensive and time-consuming. In the last years before the war, industrial expansion in the eastern areas slowed down, owing both to pressure for immediate output and complacency at the top about the ability of the Red Army to halt the enemy at the frontiers.

During the first five-year plan, while the construction of modern capital goods industries proceeded rapidly, Soviet agricultural production declined; the number of livestock fell catastrophically. A major famine occurred in 1933. Recovery was slow. In 1937–9 (average) agricultural production exceeded the 1928 level by at most 9.5 per cent, and the 1909–13 level by at most 25 per cent (Davies, Harrison and Wheatcroft 1994, tables 18, 19). In consequence agricultural production per head of population in 1937–9 was lower than in 1928 and only a few percentage points higher than in 1909–13. Within the total, the production of industrial crops increased substantially, and this enabled an increase in the output of cotton fabrics and other consumer goods based on agricultural raw materials. But, taking industrial consumer goods, manufactured foods and direct purchases of food together, total personal consumption per head of population in 1940 was estimated by a Western economist to have fallen by about 7 per cent compared with 1928 (results of Janet Chapman reported in Harrison 1994a, pp. 52–3).

One of the paradoxes of rapid industrialisation in the 1930s was that the personal consumption per head of both the urban and the rural population, considered separately, declined more rapidly than the personal consumption per head of the population as a whole. This was because a large number of people moved from the lower standard of living of the countryside to the higher standard of living of the towns; the standard of living of former peasants living in the towns increased, but the average standard of living in the towns declined.

Real wages declined much more rapidly than personal consumption – the real income per wage-earner outside agriculture may have fallen by nearly 50 per cent between 1928 and 1940. But the ending of unemployment, and the increased participation of family members (particularly married women) in the urban labour force meant that the number of wage-earners per household greatly increased. Women constituted 39 per cent of the employed labour force in 1940 compared to 24 per cent in 1928 (*Trud* 1968, p. 73). The number of dependents per wage earner fell from 2.46 in 1928 to 1.28 in 1940 (Harrison 1994a, p. 52).

While personal consumption deteriorated, state expenditure on health and education increased rapidly. Substantial growth of the social infrastructure often distinguishes industrialisation in the twentieth century from its classic predecessors; the increase in the Soviet case was particularly rapid. Employment increased even more rapidly in education than in industry (see table 11, p. 82). The number of children at school rose from 12 million in the school year 1928/9 to 35 million in the school year 1940/1. Four-year education became almost universal during the first five-year plan (1928–32), and by 1939 seven-year education (from 8+ to 14+) was almost universal in the towns. About one-third of all urban children were attending the 8–10 year school (from 14+ to 17+), but only about one-tenth of rural children. There was a $4\frac{1}{2}$-fold increase in the number of higher-education students, and the percentage of those employed in the state and co-operative sector who had received professional or semi-professional education rose from 4.6 to 7.1 per cent. Adult education was also a major feature of the 1930s – from mass literacy campaigns to special academies for the higher education of industrial managers. According to the population censuses, the percentage of literate persons in the population (from nine years of age) increased from 51 per cent in 1926 to 81 per cent in 1939. This was due partly to the higher proportion of children attending school, partly to the literacy campaign. (Fitzpatrick 1979; Davies 1989a, p. 1031.)

The social security provisions for the employed population, introduced during the 1920s, largely remained in force, accounting for some 8 per cent of the wage-bill in 1938 as compared with 10 per cent in 1930. But old-age pensions were provided only for people who had been in employment for a minimum period – at the beginning of 1941 there were only 4 million pensioners. Collective farmers counted as self-employed, and any social welfare provisions made for them had to be supplied by the collective farms (Davies 1989a, p. 1031). But labour protection measures were much less rigorously enforced in the 1930s than during NEP, particularly for women workers (Ilič 1996).

Employment in the health services increased rapidly. But the supply of medicines, medical equipment and new buildings did not increase at the same rate. In consequence the health services failed in important respects to cope with the deterioration in the conditions of life (Barber and Davies 1994, pp. 89–90; Davies 1989a, p. 1033).

In the 1930s substantial investment was undertaken in urban housing. But housing space did not increase as rapidly as the precipitate growth of the urban population: urban housing per head fell from 8.3 $m^2$ in 1926 to a mere 6.7 $m^2$ in 1940. Hardly any new housing was built in the countryside, and much of the existing rural housing stock fell into disrepair.

Forced-march industrialisation in the 1930s involved a social upheaval far greater than had occurred anywhere else in Europe in the modern era before the Second World War. The unprecedented rate of expansion of the urban population, which increased from 26 to 56 million persons between the population censuses of December 1926 and January 1939, was primarily due to migration from the countryside to the towns. Migration accounted for 62 per cent of the increase; 18 per cent was due to natural growth; and the remainder to the reclassification of former rural areas as urban (on the migration process, see Hoffman 1994).

The disruption of peasant life which accompanied industrialisation has a certain analogy with the enclosure movement in Britain. But it was compressed into a few years instead of decades or centuries. In the early 1930s, the collectivisation of agriculture required nearly all peasants to change drastically their methods of earning their living. A fairly small sector of state farms (*sovkhozy*) operated on the same principle as state factories; they employed workers who received a wage. The vast majority of peasant households were combined into some 250,000 collective farms (*kolkhozy*), one or several to each village. The old boundaries between the strips of arable land were removed. The land, producing grain and industrial crops such as sugar-beet, flax or cotton, was worked collectively. The peasant's income from the *kolkhoz* consisted of a share of the final produce; if little was produced, the peasants received little. Every peasant household also retained a personal plot worked by the family.

Some peasants in every village were forced to uproot themselves completely. 'Dekulakisation' (the expropriation of the richer *kulak* peasants) probably involved 1 million of the 25 million peasant households, 5 or 6 million persons. Over 2 million persons were exiled from their villages to remote parts of the USSR.

The vast majority of peasants suffered severe hardship – or worse – as a result of the collectivisation of agriculture and the forced requisitioning of agricultural products. The devastating famine of 1933 affected most of Ukraine, the North Caucasus and large areas of the Volga region.

Sections of the urban population also suffered imprisonment and exile. Many private traders, former nobles and merchants and their families were exiled from the towns in the early 1930s, and in the Great Purge of 1936–8 members of the Party and professional élite were arrested, and many were executed.

Before the archives were opened at the beginning of the 1990s, Western scholars made wildly varying estimates of the numbers imprisoned in the camps (see table 5). We now know that on the eve of the Second World War some 3.3 million persons were incarcerated under the control of the Gulag (the Chief Administration of Camps) (for details and sources, see Davies 1997, ch. 13; Wheatcroft 1996). There were four main categories. First, persons awaiting trial were confined in prisons. Secondly, long-term prisoners (sentenced to more than three years' confinement) were sent to labour camps (known at first as concentration camps), often located in remote areas; the term Gulag is usually used to refer to this labour camp system. Nearly all those sentenced for so-called 'counter-revolutionary' crimes were sent to labour camps. Thirdly, shorter-term prisoners (sentenced to three

Table 5 *Western pre-*glasnost' *estimates of camp population*

|  | Camp population (millions) | Year |
|---|---|---|
| Timasheff (1948) | 2.3 | end–1937 |
| Jasny (1952) | 3.5 | 1940–1 |
| Wheatcroft (1981) | 4–5 maximum[a] | 1939 |
| Swaniewicz (1965) | 6.9 | 1940–1 |
| Conquest (1968) | 9[b] | end–1938 |

*Notes:* [a] Labour camps (and colonies) only. [b] Excludes criminals, but includes political prisoners held in prisons.
*Sources:* See Wheatcroft 1996, pp. 1332–3; Conquest 1968, p. 532.

years or less) were sent to labour colonies. Fourthly, a large number of people were sent to special settlements (sometimes known as labour settlements). In the 1930s, nearly all of these were peasants classified as *kulaks* (during and after the war large numbers of Germans, Chechens and other nationalities were also sent to the special settlements). The prisons, camps and colonies contained individual prisoners who had received sentences, while whole families were often sent to the special settlements. On the eve of the war, over 80 per cent of those confined in camps were adult males, but adult males were only 30 per cent of those in special settlements. All adults classified as fit were required to work, in the camps, colonies and special settlements. The approximate total number of prisoners is shown in table 6.

Table 6 *Total number of prisoners in the forced labour system, 1933–53*

|  | (1 January of each year; in thousands) | | | |
|---|---|---|---|---|
|  | 1933 | 1937 | 1941 | 1953 |
| Prisons | 800 | 545 | 488 | 276 |
| Camps | 334 | 821 | 1501 | 1728 |
| Colonies | 240 | 375 | 420 | 741 |
| Special settlements | 1142 | 917 | 930 | 2754 |
| Total | 2516 | 2658 | 3339 | 5499 |

*Sources:* See Davies 1997, p. 166.

These figures do not cover all those subject to repression. Thus some people were exiled from the big towns without being confined in a settlement; some people who had been released from camps were not permitted to return to their place of origin. The numbers in these categories are not known.

How large a contribution did the Gulag system make to economic development? Of the total of 3.3 million people in 1941, two million or so were working in various sectors of the economy. The prisoners were most important for capital construction, and provided up to a quarter of all building labour. Over vast areas of the Urals, Siberia and the Far East it was the Gulag which was primarily responsible for the construction of mines, factories and railways.

On the eve of the war, only about 1.2 per cent of gross industrial output was produced by Gulag labour. But forced labour was important in certain industries in remote areas, especially in the production of gold and some non-ferrous metals (after the war prisoners were widely used in the production of atomic bombs). About 12 per cent of timber and firewood was produced by Gulag labour.

The use of forced labour in the Stalin system was a form of forced saving: prisoners could be allocated to work under terrible conditions in remote areas where free workers would be unwilling to go without very large increases in wages. But it is not at all clear whether, even from a narrowly economic point of view, the economic 'gains' were outweighed by the costs and inefficiencies of this inhuman system. Swaniewicz pointed out many years ago that the lower productivity of forced labour, and the high cost of maintaining the machinery of coercion, at least partly offset the 'savings' received by the regime from cheap labour (Swaniewicz 1965, pp. 189–207).

During these years of upheaval and deprivation millions of people died prematurely. How many is not precisely known, largely because we do not know how many of the children who died during the famine years remained entirely unregistered. Serious estimates of excess deaths between the censuses of 1926 and 1939 range from 7 to 14 million. On all estimates most of these deaths occurred during the 1932–3 famine. Many other people died of malnutrition, disease and neglect in the camps and settlements of the Gulag system. And many people were sentenced to death: according to the official records, which are incomplete, 739,000 persons were executed for 'counter-revolutionary and other particularly dangerous state crimes' in the period 1927–41, as many as 682,000 of these in the two years 1937 and 1938. (Wheatcroft and Davies 1994b, pp. 67–77.)

The human catastrophe of the 1930s, unlike the deaths resulting from the two world wars, did not result in an absolute decline in the population, which increased by 19–20 million between 1926 and 1939. But the repression and social upheaval of the 1930s postponed the long-term trend towards the improvement of life expectancy and health. Infant mortality (deaths between 0 and 1 year of age) fell from 273 to 174 per thousand live births between 1913 and 1927; but it failed to improve in the 1930s, amounting to 167 per thousand in 1939 and 182 in 1940 (Barber and Davies 1994, p. 90; Davies, Harrison and Wheatcroft 1994, p. 276).

## Sub-phases of economic development, 1928–41

In the period 1928–41, the economy went through many vicissitudes. Five main phases may be distinguished.

*(1) 1928–30.* Industrialisation, with a strong emphasis on the capital goods industries, proceeded at an accelerating pace. The successive drafts of the first five-year plan and the annual plans became increasingly ambitious. The climax was reached when the XVIth Party Congress in July 1930 approved very high five-year plan targets for key industries. These targets were reached not in the economic year 1932/3 as planned, but some years after the Second World War.

In 1928 and 1929 the use of state coercion, including the widespread use of violence, replaced the market relation with the peasants; the 'emergency measures' of the beginning of 1928 became a permanent feature of the system. From the autumn of 1929, the forcible collectivisation of agriculture strengthened state control over agricultural output. Collectivisation was accompanied by the mass deportation of *kulak* households; heads of households believed to be particularly dangerous were summarily executed.

The simultaneous increase of industrial production and capital construction involved the rapid expansion of the industrial and building labour force. To meet the higher national wage-bill, the flow of paper money was increased. Prices began to rise, but inflation was partly suppressed through price controls; private shops and trading agencies were taken over by the state to facilitate this. With the breakdown of the market in 1929 a rationing system was introduced in the towns; following the practices of the Civil War, rations were differentiated by occupation. Rationing continued until 1935. As in the Civil War, food was also sold extensively by the peasants on the free market – partly legally, partly illegally – at much higher prices. In this way, the available supply of consumer goods and food was distributed over the old and the new urban population, and consumption per head in the towns was forced down.

Within industry, a rudimentary system of physical controls already existed in the 1920s. This was gradually extended in the period 1928–30, so that virtually all capital goods and raw materials were physically allocated. In industry – and in the towns generally – many 'bourgeois' engineers, economists and other specialists who were suspected of resisting party policies, or even of insufficient enthusiasm, were arrested and accused of sabotage (see Bailes 1978; Lampert 1979).

In this period, Utopian concepts of the emerging Socialist order prevailed in official circles. During the collectivisation drive of January–March 1930, attempts were made to socialise all livestock and close down peasant markets. Leading economists and officials announced that the transition to socialism would soon be completed; this would involve a moneyless economy, in which trade would be replaced by physical product exchange (exchange in kind, or barter).

*(2) Spring/summer 1930–summer 1932.* Economic policy and practice were confused and ambiguous. On the one hand, feverish attempts continued throughout 1931 and 1932 to achieve the over-ambitious plans approved in July 1930. By 1932 the number of people employed in large-scale industry had more than doubled, and the number employed in construction quadrupled, as compared with 1928. Currency continued to be issued in large

quantities to provide finance for this expansion. But industrial projects took much longer to complete than planned, and the strain placed on industry by the over-ambitious plans led to much disorder. In consequence, industrial production grew less rapidly in 1931 and 1932 than in previous years.

In agriculture, widespread peasant disturbances in February 1930 compelled a temporary retreat from collectivisation; but both the relentless collectivisation drive and dekulakisation were resumed at the end of 1930. By the end of 1932, over 60 per cent of all peasant households had joined the *kolkhozy* (collective farms). The state continued to compel both collective farms and individual households to surrender very large quantities of grain and other products, for a purely nominal payment, and offered virtually no economic inducement to the peasants to work on collective land.

So far the policies we have described involved no important departure from the previous period. But in the course of 1930–2 greater realism gradually came to prevail. As early as the spring of 1930, at the time of the retreat from collectivisation, Stalin called a halt to the compulsory socialisation of all livestock, and to the attempts to eliminate the peasant free market. In the autumn of the same year the flirtation with the moneyless economy was abandoned in favour of a policy of strengthening the ruble and strict financial discipline, though this could not be put into effect while the ambitious plans continued. From the spring of 1931 the authorities relinquished their enthusiasm for product exchange in kind, and began to insist on the necessity for 'Soviet trade' and on the eventual need to abolish consumer rationing. Simultaneously the pressure on 'bourgeois specialists' was relaxed, though never completely removed. In May 1932 the free peasant market (the so-called 'collective-farm (*kolkhoz*) market') was legalised. Collective farmers and individual peasants were allowed to sell, at free-market prices, the produce which remained after they had handed over their compulsory deliveries to the state. These sales on the market (for what the peasant could get) became a major source of peasant income. At the same time the compulsory delivery quotas imposed on agriculture were reduced, and strenuous efforts were made to provide economic incentives to the collective farms. Taken together these measures were unofficially known as 'neo-NEP'.

*(3) 1933.*   The measures of relaxation in the spring of 1932 were too little and too late. Following a poor harvest in 1932, the peasants failed to meet even their reduced delivery quotas. In the winter of 1932–3 the state pursued the grain quotas with particular brutality; recalcitrant households were exiled. A terrible famine followed in the spring of 1933; millions of peasants died from starvation. The poor condition of agriculture in 1932 was undoubtedly in large part the result of the excesses of collectivisation and the size of the food quotas imposed on the peasants. Was poverty turned into disaster by the deliberate actions of Stalin, in his determination to force the peasants to submit to the requirements of the state? Or was Stalin impelled to enforce the food quotas because the desperate food situation in the towns threatened the whole process of industrialisation? No agreement has been reached by historians on this grim topic.

In the economy at large, the authorities committed themselves to more realistic policies. The production plan for 1933 was much more modest than in previous years, and the level of investment was actually reduced for the first time since the early 1920s. The 1933 plan, and the draft second five-year plan (covering 1933–7) stressed that top priority should be given to completing investment projects started during the first five-year plan, and assimilating them into production. Budgetary expenditure was curbed, and in consequence the amount of currency in circulation declined in 1933.

*(4) 1934–6.*   This was a period of spectacular economic development. Many of the factories started during the first five-year plan were brought into operation, and agriculture began to recover from crisis. According to an American estimate, gross national product (GNP) increased by about 55 per cent between 1932 and 1937 (see table 10, p. 82). Labour productivity rose substantially in agriculture as well as industry. The standard of living improved greatly, from the low level of 1933. In 1935 all consumer rationing was abolished.

This was also a period of growing differentiation in living standards and way of life between the privileged élite and the mass of the population. Within the working class the pay differentials for highly productive workers were considerably increased (see

Siegelbaum 1988). And greater prosperity did not carry with it relaxation of repression, except for a brief period in 1934. Following the assassination in December 1934 of Kirov, a prominent member of the Politburo, many Party members, as well as those outside the Party, were arrested and executed. The first major public trial of Old Bolsheviks was held in August 1936. The international scene was grim and foreboding. Following the Japanese invasion of Manchuria in September 1931 and the seizure of power by the Nazis in Germany in January 1933, tension grew throughout Europe and Asia; in response Soviet military expenditure increased. In the period 1934–6 a considerable strain was placed upon the economy by the need to modernise weapons and production processes in the armaments industry in face of the military threat (Harrison and Davies 1997).

*(5) 1937–22 June 1941.*  These years were haunted by the political purges, involving in 1937–8 mass arrests of leading economic officials and industrial managers. In Europe, tension mounted: the outbreak of the Spanish Civil War in July 1936 was followed by the invasion of Austria in March 1938 and the dismemberment of Czechoslovakia later in the year. Soviet war preparations greatly intensified. The armed forces expanded from 1.5 million in 1937 to over 5 million on the eve of the German invasion, while armaments production increased at a similar rate: in 1940 it was nearly $2\frac{1}{2}$ times as great as in 1937. And by 1937, consequent upon the high levels of investment during the previous three years, the economy entered a new crisis of overaccumulation, similar to, though less acute, than the crisis of 1931–2. In 1938–40, as in the first years of the second five-year plan, considerable efforts were devoted to completing unfinished projects. Purges, rearmament and overaccumulation together resulted in a considerable slowing down of the growth of industry.

Economic policy was dominated by the rearmament drive, particularly intensive from 1939. The large increases in defence expenditure had repercussions throughout the economy. Purchasing power rose more rapidly than state retail sales. In consequence, prices on the collective-farm free market rose considerably, and in 1940 and 1941 official retail prices were also increased. Numerous austerity measures were introduced to restrict budget expenditure for civilian purposes. The working day was lengthened, and labour discipline was tightened up.

## The effectiveness of forced industrialisation in the pre-war years

How effective was the forced industrialisation drive in these tumultuous years? It has not proved possible to devise any reliable quantitative measure of efficiency. General measures of the efficiency of an economy or of one of its sectors are based on a 'production function', which compares the rate of growth of output and the rate of growth of inputs, particularly capital and labour. That part of the growth of output which cannot be attributed to the growth of inputs is taken as a measure of efficiency; it is referred to as total factor productivity (or alternatively as 'the residual', the amount which remains after the rate of growth of the combined inputs is deducted from the rate of growth of output). Many technical difficulties complicate the task of estimating production functions for any economy. In a Soviet-type economy the absence of capital and labour markets makes it particularly difficult to determine the relative weights to be attributed to the inputs.

But the greatest problem is that, as we have already seen, estimates of the basic Soviet economic quantities for the years 1928–40 vary widely. Only the rate of growth of labour inputs is known with some certainty. Measurements of the annual rate of growth of gross and net national product (GNP and NNP – see Glossary) and of the rate of growth of capital vary considerably. In consequence Western estimates of the share of total factor productivity in the growth of GNP/NNP vary from 2 to 24 per cent (Lewis 1994b, pp. 192–7, tables 41, 42). In the industrial sector even quite high estimates of the rate of growth of production lead to the conclusion that total factor productivity accounted for only 12–19 per cent of the growth of large-scale industry between 1928 and 1937, and that almost all this increase took place after 1933 (Lewis 1994b, pp. 192–7, tables 41, 42). It is tempting to see these results as confirming the commonsense view that substantial increases in efficiency were unlikely to have occurred in this period of economic upheaval and social disorder.

In the absence of reliable quantitative assessments, we have to turn to more general considerations of effectiveness. In Western discussions most attention has naturally been devoted to the relationship between industry and agriculture. The collectivisation of agriculture, accompanied as it was by state requisitions of a large part of agricultural output, failed to increase yield or total production. But were collectivisation and requisitioning effective means of transferring resources to industrialisation?

Until the early 1970s almost all Western historians assumed that agriculture was the main source of labour and capital for industry, and that collectivisation was the crucial though brutal mechanism by which this was achieved. Three achievements were particularly emphasised. First, the increase in compulsory delivery of grain to the state. In 1938–40, deliveries averaged 30 million tonnes from an average harvest of some 77 million tonnes (39 per cent), as compared with 10.7 million out of 73 million tonnes in 1928 (14.7 per cent). Secondly, the increased production of cotton and other products which were previously imported saved foreign currency and provided essential materials for industry. Thirdly, the agricultural sector provided most of the increase in urban labour. The scale of the migration was a consequence of state pressure on the peasants and the deterioration of conditions in the countryside, together with the lure of ample employment in the towns. This was not due to deliberate state policy; it was rather an unintended consequence of the priorities of the central authorities. But it greatly facilitated the increase in industrial production and in construction generally.

This positive view of the effects of collectivisation has been strongly challenged by Barsov, a Soviet economic historian, and by James Millar. Barsov claimed that the terms of trade for agriculture did not deteriorate during 1928–32, and improved in the period 1933–7. While some agricultural commodities, especially grain, were transferred to the state at low prices, others were sold on the free market at high prices; in physical terms, while the supply of grain by the peasants increased, their supply of meat and dairy products declined. Thus peasants' money incomes were higher and their supplies to the town lower than was previously believed. On the side of supply to the peasants from the towns, their high money earnings enabled them to buy industrial consumer goods. Agriculture also received greatly increased supplies of machinery from industry through state-owned Machine-Tractor Stations (MTS), each of which served the surrounding collective farms with a pool of tractors, combine harvesters and other machinery. On average each MTS served some thirty collective farms. The total flow of industrial products to the countryside, in the form of both consumer goods and machinery, was therefore higher than previously believed.

Other economists, while concurring with much of this general account, do not accept its implications. The late Professor Alec Nove argued that, in the circumstances of forced industrialisation, the state could not have obtained increased supplies of agricultural products without a drastic shift in the terms of trade in favour of agriculture (thus he rejected Millar's view of peasant behaviour in response to prices). Nove also pointed out that food and other consumption declined more rapidly in the countryside than in the towns, so that in this sense peasants made a major sacrifice for industrialisation. Collectivisation also enabled agriculture to be treated as a residual sector, which absorbed shocks such as bad harvests (for this controversy, see Millar and Nove 1976; Harrison 1980).

Whatever the outcome of this controversy, it seems clear that collectivisation of agriculture, together with the suppression of autonomous working-class activity in industry, and the repressive measures against the professional classes, provided a framework which imposed the economic priorities of the party leaders on the whole of society. In this broader sense it formed part, though a costly part, of the Stalinist mechanism for industrialisation.


## The Second World War, 1941–1945

The ultimate Soviet justification for industrialising at such a breakneck speed was that armed attack from an economically superior capitalist power was inevitable. 'We are 50–100 years behind the advanced countries', Stalin stated in a famous speech of 4 February 1931. 'We must close this gap in ten years. Either we achieve this, or they will do us in.' When Nazi Germany invaded the Soviet Union ten years and four months later, this comment acquired a prophetic quality.

Soviet industrialisation was certainly directed towards the establishment of a powerful armaments industry. Between 1930 and 1940 the total production of the defence sector of industry (including the consumer goods produced by the sector) increased twenty-eight-fold, several times more rapidly than industry as a whole (Davies, Harrison and Wheatcroft 1994, p. 299). Perhaps even more important than the construction of a modern armaments industry was the rapid expansion of the iron and steel, non-ferrous metals, fuel and power, chemicals and machine-building industries, and the training of engineers and skilled industrial workers. Without these, the munitions industry could not have existed, still less could it have greatly expanded during the years of war. 'The outcome of the war', according to Harrison, 'is to be explained primarily by reference to the ability of the opposing sides to produce munitions in wartime' (Harrison 1990b, p. 68).

But in important respects Soviet economic power proved inadequate to the test of war. Germany and her allies succeeded in occupying territory on which one-third of Soviet industrial capacity and as much as one-half of all armaments capacity had been located on the eve of the war. In 1941–2 key factories and personnel were evacuated eastwards in an operation of huge scope and urgency. But the capital evacuated amounted to a little over one-third of the total industrial capacity on enemy-occupied territory. Two-thirds – 20 per cent of all Soviet industrial capacity – was left behind. (Harrison 1994b, pp. 252–4.) Some, like the Dnieper dam, was destroyed.

The pre-war eastward relocation of industry, though substantial, had proved insufficient. In the later 1930s the Soviet authorities – especially Stalin himself – convinced themselves that invading forces would be rebuffed at the frontiers, and failed to maintain the expensive effort to relocate industry.

The rapidity of the German advance – in the course of which several million Soviet soldiers were taken prisoner – revealed profound weaknesses in the Soviet political system. The human consequences of industrialisation had undermined the morale of large sections of the population, especially in the countryside. But many of the weaknesses in morale cannot be attributed to industrialisation. A major part was played by the repression of large numbers of senior army officers, engineers and scientists – many of whom had been executed. Their repression cannot plausibly be explained by any economic factor, and the damage which this and other features of the Stalinist system caused to the Soviet ability to resist must be explained in other terms.

The year of greatest danger was 1942, when the enemy armies made their furthest inroads into Soviet territory. In 1942, 11 million men and women were serving in the Soviet armed forces, as compared with 5 million at the time of the German invasion. The heavy losses in the first stages of the war (soldiers killed in battle, dead of wounds, or taken prisoner) meant that as many as 16 or 17 million people had to be recruited from the civilian economy in the first eighteen months of war in order to reach and maintain an army of 11-million (Harrison 1994b, p. 257).

As a consequence of loss of territory, manpower and capital, GNP declined in 1942 to a mere 66 per cent of the pre-war level. Industrial output fell by 14 per cent (table 7). Occupied territory included not only one-third of industrial capacity but also areas which in 1940 produced 40 per cent of grain and virtually all sugar, and maintained 40 per cent of cattle. The countryside in Soviet territory was denuded of able-bodied men, who had been recruited for the army. In 1942 agricultural output fell to 40 per

Table 7 *Gross national product by sector of origin, 1940–5*

|  | (Billion rubles at 1937 factor cost) | | | | | |
|  | 1940 | 1941 | 1942 | 1943 | 1944 | 1945 |
|---|---|---|---|---|---|---|
| Agriculture | 69.9 | 44.1 | 27.4 | 30.5 | 45.1 | 47.3 |
| Industry | 75.1 | 73.3 | 64.8 | 75.7 | 84.9 | 71.9 |
| *Defence* | *10.5* | *16.8* | *38.7* | *47.8* | *52.3* | *36.7* |
| *Civilian* | *64.5* | *56.5* | *26.1* | *27.8* | *32.6* | *35.2* |
| Construction | 10.6 | 6.9 | 3.2 | 3.4 | 4.4 | 4.5 |
| Military services | 7.9 | 11.1 | 17.4 | 18.2 | 18.7 | 18.6 |
| Other | 90.4 | 83.3 | 54.0 | 57.6 | 67.2 | 66.8 |
| Total | 253.9 | 218.7 | 166.8 | 185.4 | 220.3 | 209.1 |

*Note:* 'Other' includes depreciation.
*Source:* Harrison 1996, p. 92.

Table 8 *Defence outlays as percentage of GNP, 1940–4*

|  | 1940 | 1941 | 1942 | 1943 | 1944 |
|---|---|---|---|---|---|
| Total defence outlays | 17 | 28 | 61 | 61 | 53 |
| Net defence imports (mainly Lend-Lease) | 0 | 0 | 5 | 10 | 10 |
| Total defence outlays less net imports | 17 | 28 | 56 | 51 | 43 |
| Non-defence outlays | 83 | 72 | 44 | 49 | 57 |
| Total GNP | 100 | 100 | 100 | 100 | 100 |

*Source:* Harrison 1996, p. 110.

cent of the 1940 level (table 7). But the population of the Soviet-controlled areas had fallen by only one-third. The decline in agricultural output was far greater than that during the Civil War. Widespread hunger and malnutrition resulted, in spite of the enforcement of a food rationing system which seems to have been more efficient than the rationing arrangements of both the Civil War and the early 1930s.

In spite of these tremendous losses, the rigorous direction of resources enabled the production of munitions in 1942 to reach three times the 1940 level. Table 8 includes in 'defence outlays' the inputs into munitions production and the other defence sectors from civilian industry, transport, agriculture, and so on. By 1942, the shape of the economy had completely changed: the defence sector had increased from 17 per cent to an astonishing 56 per cent of a substantially lower GNP.

The amount of national income available for non-defence purposes declined from 210 billion rubles in 1940 to 73 billion rubles in 1942, just over a third of the pre-war level. The Soviet Union mobilised at least as great a share of its national income for military purposes as Britain, and a greater share than the United States. This is an even more remarkable performance than these proportions indicate. The national income per capita was much higher in Britain and the United States; and they achieved their mobilisation of resources from a rising total wartime national income, while in the Soviet Union national income greatly declined. (For the data in the above three paragraphs, see Harrison 1996.)

The huge shift to the production of armaments did not merely involve the more intensive use of existing capacity in armaments factories – often after their relocation a thousand miles or more to the east. During the 1930s successive 'mobilisation plans' for civilian factories had made preparations for their conversion to military purposes. But in the strained circumstances of 1942 conversion went much further than the mobilisation plans had envisaged and involved heroic improvisation. An account of the Soviet home front offers striking examples, all taken from Moscow alone: 'A children's bicycle factory began making flame-throwers. A die-stamping works where teaspoons and paper clips were made switched to entrenching tools and parts for anti-tank grenades. A woodworking shop producing abacuses and screens changed over to making pistol cartridges ... A typewriter works began making automatic rifles and ammunition' (Barber and Harrison 1991, p. 135).

The defence effort involved an unprecedented degree of mobilisation of the labour force. Between 1940 and 1942, the total supply of labour declined by 32 million persons, but the number of persons involved in the war effort increased by 14 million – 6 million extra in the armed forces, 8 million extra in war work. This meant that numbers employed outside the defence sector – mainly in agriculture – declined by as many as 46 million, from 73 to 27 million (Harrison 1996, p. 122). Forced labour continued to be employed extensively in the economy. In 1942 some $1^{1}/_{2}$ million or so of the $2^{1}/_{2}$ million prisoners in camps, colonies and special settlements were engaged in forced labour, mainly in construction, mining and timber, as compared with a total non-agricultural labour force of some 18 million persons (see Bacon 1994, ch. 7).

These exertions provided the basis for the Soviet defeat of the German armies in November 1942 at Stalingrad and for the Soviet victory in 1943 in the battle of Kursk, in which Soviet tanks proved superior in number and equal in quality to the most modern German tanks.

In the remaining years of the war, 1943 and 1944, the output of munitions continued to increase, reaching nearly four times the 1940 level in the latter year. But the expansion of the national income, partly a consequence of the liberation of occupied territory, meant that the amount of national income for civilian purposes could also expand. By 1944 it had reached 103 billion rubles, though this was still less than half of the pre-war level.

An important contribution was made to the Soviet war effort by foreign assistance, almost entirely American Lend-Lease. These supplies were not significant before the Battle of Stalingrad in 1942. But they reached their peak in 1943 and 1944, when they amounted to as much as 10 per cent of gross national product, and undoubtedly played a part in the rapid rout of the enemy. Substantial amounts of food were provided, but the bulk of the supplies consisted of armaments and industrial materials. The Soviet Union produced all of its own artillery, seven-eighths of its own tanks and armoured vehicles, and five-sixths of its own aircraft. But it was heavily dependent on the United States for lorries and jeeps, and field telephones. (Harrison 1985, pp. 256–66; Barber and Harrison 1991, pp. 189–90.)

The human cost of the Soviet victory, finally achieved in May 1945, was immense. The population declined from 197 million in June 1941 to only 171 million at the end of 1945. Demographers have estimated that during the war some 26 million Soviet citizens died prematurely, and a further 14 million were not born owing to the precipitate decline in the birth rate. The breakdown of the 26 million war deaths is known only approximately. Some 8–9 million soldiers were killed or died of wounds or disease; 0.8 million civilians died in the siege of Leningrad. According to one estimate, 11 million of the remaining 17 million died on German-occupied territory; $2\frac{1}{2}$ million of these were Jews murdered by Nazi exterminators. An unknown number of persons died on Soviet territory in the Gulag system, including many of over 3 million Soviet Germans, Chechens and other nationalities deported in 1940–5. But the overwhelming majority of civilian deaths must have been a result of illness, malnourishment and ill-treatment on occupied territory, in captivity in German-occupied Europe, and in the harsh conditions of the Soviet civilian rear. Excess deaths amounted to 18 million during the First World War, the Civil War and their aftermath, and some 10 million in the 1930s. So the 26 million deaths in 1941–5 constituted the worst of the three demographic catastrophes which the Russian

Empire and the Soviet Union suffered during the twentieth century.

## Post-war recovery, 1945–1950

In 1945 much of the Soviet Union lay in ruins. The major European industrial and agricultural areas had been occupied by the enemy; and although the capital equipment of many factories had been evacuated, the destruction in the occupied areas was very extensive. On the best estimate, one-quarter of all national wealth had been destroyed (Harrison 1996, pp. 157–9). And one-third of young males had been killed. At the time of the 1959 population census, nearly 14 years after the end of the war, there were over 20 million more females than males in the USSR, and 14.8 million of these were between 30 and 59 years of age (so they had been 16–45 years old in 1945). And at the end of the war 25 million people were homeless.

Agriculture had been particularly devastated by the war. Total agricultural production had fallen by one-third; the grain harvest in 1945 was a mere 47 million tonnes, a lower amount per head of population even than in the famine year 1921. The civilian production of industry had also declined according to official figures by at least one-third (and on a Western estimate, by nearly three-fifths). But as a result of the vast expansion of armaments production, total industrial production in 1945 was still between 70 per cent (Western estimate) and 90 per cent (Soviet estimate) of the 1940 level. In contrast, in 1920 at the end of the First World War and the Civil War industrial production had fallen to a mere 20 per cent of the pre-war level. In 1941–5 more human beings were destroyed than in 1914–20, but less industry.

The first stages of recovery after 1945 were naturally extremely painful. The huge problems of restoring the shattered regions were compounded by the bad harvest of 1946, which was primarily a result of the unfavourable weather: grain production fell to a mere 40 million tonnes, less than in 1945. Famine conditions prevailed in many regions; according to a recent Russian estimate, deaths from hunger and from illness due to famine in 1947 amounted to at least 1 million (Zima 1993, pp. 42–4).

Table 9 *Gross military and civil industrial production, 1940–7*

| | (Billion rubles at 1926/7 prices; Soviet official figures) | | | | |
| | 1940 | 1944 | 1945 | 1946 | 1947 |
|---|---|---|---|---|---|
| Civilian | 115 | 69 | 76 | 92 | 115 |
| Military | 24 | 75 | 50 | 14 | 14 |
| Total | 139 | 144 | 127 | 107 | 129 |

*Sources:* Davies, Harrison and Wheatcroft 1994, p. 241; Russian archives.

The transition from war to peace involved the rapid large-scale conversion of armaments factories to civilian production, and the reconversion to their original use of civilian factories where armaments had been produced during the war. The decline in armaments production in 1946 was so considerable that total production fell, and did not recover to the 1945 level until the following year (see table 9).

After these initial difficulties, recovery – as in the case of some other industrial economies devastated by war – was rapid. By the end of the fourth five-year plan (1946–50) industrial production considerably exceeded, and agricultural production slightly exceeded, the pre-war level (see table 10, p. 82).

Some contribution to recovery was made by reparations from the former enemy countries, particularly Germany. These took the form of both materials and equipment; in addition, joint corporations were established on former enemy soil, from which the Soviet Union obtained materials and profit. The size of the reparations contribution is still disputed. A careful American estimate suggests that it amounted to about 1.5 per cent of GNP in 1948–50 (Bergson 1961, p.100, compared with GNP figures in Moorsteen and Powell 1966, p. 623). Other estimates are higher (see the discussion in Goldman 1967, pp. 3–22). But reparations were certainly a small proportion of the losses suffered by the Soviet Union as a result of the invasion.

To achieve recovery the Soviet authorities resumed the economic policies of the 1930s. In 1945, gross investment in fixed capital had fallen to two-thirds of the 1940 level; in 1946–50 it increased by as much as 21 per cent a year, far more rapidly than the growth of national income, and by 1950 was 70 per cent higher than in 1940 (estimated from data in 1937 prices in Moorsteen and Powell 1966, p. 358). Within total investment, the capital goods industries again received the highest priority. In 1950 the production of oil, coal, electricity and steel in each case considerably exceeded the planned target, and was considerably higher than in 1940. According to the official Soviet index, the production of capital goods (including armaments) in 1950 was as much as 105 per cent above the 1940 level; but even according to a conservative Western estimate, the increase amounted to 82 per cent (Nutter 1962, p. 524; all finished civilian products except consumer goods; 1955 prices). In these recovery years, armaments production was not a major drain on production. After the precipitate decline in 1944–7, it increased by nearly 40 per cent in 1947–50, less than half as rapidly as industry as a whole.

In sharp contrast to the successful expansion of the capital goods industries, the plans for the consumer goods industries were not fulfilled. The production of cotton textiles barely reached the 1940 level, and the production of linen textiles and footwear was lower than in 1940. According to the official Soviet index, consumer goods production in 1950 exceeded the 1940 level by 23 per cent; but according to a Western estimate, the increase was only 8 per cent (Nutter 1962, pp. 527–8; 1955 weights).

Within the consumer goods sector, by far the most rapid expansion was in the production of consumer durables, which reached 250 per cent of the 1940 level by 1950 (Nutter 1962, pp. 527–8; 1955 weights). Consumer durables, from iron bedsteads to radios and clocks and watches, were largely produced in engineering and armaments factories, and benefited from their relatively advanced technology. But the consumer industries in large part depended for their expansion on the success of agriculture, which supplied grain, meat, milk and sugar for the food industry, and cotton, wool and linen for the textile industries. Agriculture lagged far behind industry. According to the official index, in 1950 it was still slightly below the pre-war level. Grain production reached only 81 million tonnes, 14 million less than in 1940. In these last years of the Stalin period, grain production per head of population was substantially lower than in 1913; and this had a profound effect on the general standard of living of the population.

This failure did not result from the complete neglect of agriculture. In these post-war years, the production of tractors and combine harvesters increased rapidly, and by 1950 was substantially greater than in the pre-war peak year 1936 (in 1937–40 agricultural machinery factories were extensively converted to the production of tanks and other military equipment). In spite of wartime destruction, the total stock of tractors, combine harvesters and lorries used in agriculture substantially exceeded the pre-war level by 1950 (*Narodnoe khozyaistvo* 1959, p. 487). But agriculture was now supported by an ageing and largely female unskilled labour force: many young men from the villages were killed during the war, and many others failed to return to work on the land, and many young women also left the villages for work in the towns. Life and work in the villages was far less attractive than life and work in the towns. The villages lacked amenities; and the collective farmers received a very poor return for their work. State payments per tonne for the compulsory delivery of grain and other agricultural products were extremely low. While retail prices of the commodities purchased by peasants were at least ten times the 1928 level in 1952, the state payments for wheat had increased by only 19 per cent; state payments kept pace with retail prices only in the case of cotton, flax and other industrial crops (Malafeev 1964, p. 267).

The education system recovered slowly from the effects of the war. The pre-war achievement of providing education for nearly all urban children and half the rural children to the age of fifteen was restored by 1950. But in 1950 the number of children in grades VIII–X (15–17 year olds) was substantially below the 1940 level; and this shortfall was only partly compensated by the increase in the number of teenagers attending specialised secondary schools and technical colleges (*Kul'turnoe stroitel'stvo* 1956, pp. 76–159). The higher education of a relatively small élite expanded far more rapidly: the number of new graduates in 1950 amounted to 177,000 as compared with 126,000 in 1940 (*Kul'turnoe stroitel'stvo* 1956, p. 204).

## Post-war expansion, 1950–1965

The 1950s and the early 1960s were the golden years of the Soviet administrative economy. Even before Stalin's death in March

1953 certain tentative signs of a major shift in economic policy had appeared. Between 1950 and 1952, the production of consumer goods increased almost as rapidly as that of capital goods (according to official figures, by 28 against 31 per cent) (Clarke 1972, pp. 8–9). For the first time since 1940 influential articles in the Soviet economic press stressed the importance of *khozraschet* (profit-and-loss accounting) and other economic incentives (Miller 1952/3, pp. 447–68; Davies 1955/6, pp. 451–4). The tight controls over the movement of labour introduced on the eve of and during the war were somewhat relaxed (Barker[1955], p. 99). Far-reaching plans provided for the expansion of agriculture.

But until 1953 no fundamental shift took place in economic policy. In agriculture, taxation was even increased, and the supply of tractors declined. The plans for agricultural expansion failed utterly. The use of forced labour was even extended in Stalin's last years: the number of persons in prisons, camps, colonies and special settlements (including family members) reached a record 5,499,000 on 1 January 1953; 2,754,000 of these were families in special settlements, mainly national minorities deported for alleged disloyalty during and at the end of the war (Davies 1997, p. 166).

The economy of the early 1950s had undergone fundamental changes as compared with the late 1920s. Agriculture was responsible for 47 per cent of GNP in 1928, industry for only 20 per cent. By 1955, the share of agriculture had fallen to 20 per cent, and that of industry had risen to 37 per cent (see table 10, p. 82).

In the course of this transformation the state-employed labour force rapidly increased, and the number of well-qualified personnel increased even more rapidly. In 1928, some 5 per cent of the employed labour force had received professional or semi-professional education; by 1955, the proportion had increased to 11 per cent, although the number of persons employed by the state was over four times as large. (The percentage continued to increase, reaching 16 per cent in 1965 and 30 per cent in 1987.)

The increase in the proportion of women in the labour force which took place during the Second World War remained a permanent feature of the Soviet economy. By 1945 56 per cent of the total employed labour force were women, as compared with 39 per cent in 1940; and the figure remained as high as 50 per cent in

1966 (*Trud* 1968, p. 73). Women now played a major role in some professions which had previously been largely male: in 1965 women were 30 per cent of all graduate engineers as compared with 15 per cent in 1940 (estimate from data in *Trud* 1968, pp. 268–9, 274–5). But within each trade or profession women on the whole tended to occupy the less skilled and less responsible posts, so women's average earnings remained substantially lower than men's.

As we have seen, the industrial advance was one-sided. Most progress had been made in certain capital goods industries: for example, armaments, some branches of machine-building including machine-tools, and the iron and steel industry. Other capital goods industries, including chemicals, were far more backward, as were most consumer goods industries. And agriculture was the Achilles' heel of the economy: although much mechanisation had taken place, the yields and the productivity of labour were still extremely low.

After 1953 the new leaders introduced major changes in economic priorities. Investment in agriculture was sharply increased, and by 1958 reached 250 per cent of the 1953 level. Much of this investment was directed to the provision of tractors and other machinery for the expansion of the area sown to grain in the 'Virgin Lands' of northern Kazakhstan, southern Siberia and south-east European Russia. The total area sown to grain increased by 17 per cent during the period 1953–7. (Nove 1982, pp. 332–3, 336.) Simultaneously the prices paid by the state for agricultural products were very substantially increased: as a result the money incomes of collective farms more than doubled between 1953 and 1958. Increased investment and improved prices were accompanied by a rapid rise in agricultural output, which increased by 55 per cent between 1950 and 1960, twice the growth rate in the whole period 1928–60. Grain production increased from 81 million tonnes in 1950 to 126 million in 1960; nearly three-quarters of this increase came from the Virgin Lands.

Other important changes in economic policy included a substantial increase in the share of investment devoted to urban housing construction; and a relative and absolute increase in resources devoted to consumer goods. Between 1950 and 1965 the stock of urban housing more than doubled; and the gap between the rates of growth of the production of capital and consumer goods was much narrower than in the 1930s.

All this meant that the standard of living of the mass of the population increased substantially for the first time since the 1920s. Other important changes also bettered the lot of many ordinary citizens. Health provisions greatly improved; the crude death rate declined from 18 per thousand population in 1940 to 9.7 in 1950 and 7.3 in 1965. The infant mortality rate is perhaps the best indicator of the improvement in health: it had already fallen from 182 per thousand live births in 1940 to 81 in 1950, and by 1965 it was only 27 per thousand.

There was a similar improvement in the level of education. The number of pupils in the top four classes (14+ to 17+) rose from 1.8 million in the school year 1950/1 to 12.7 million in 1965/6. And the number of students in higher education trebled in the same period, from 1.25 to 3.86 million. Paradoxically, the better-educated young people of the 1960s – one of the major successes of the Communist system – played a major part (perhaps *the* major part) in the struggle to reform the system in the second half of the 1980s; the failure of the system to accommodate to them was a major factor in its downfall.

In the first few years after Stalin's death the Gulag system was largely dismantled. The number of persons confined to camps, colonies and special settlements (these figures do not include prisons) fell from 5,223,000 on 1 January 1953 to 997,000 on 1 January 1959; within this total, the number imprisoned as so-called 'counter-revolutionaries' declined from 580,000 to only 11,000 (Davies 1997, p. 183). The fear which loomed over large sections of the population was at least mitigated.

A significant shift also took place in the distribution of income. The incomes of peasants, extremely low in 1953, increased much more rapidly than those of the urban population. Within the urban population, there was a process of levelling-up: the minimum wage was increased, wage differentials were narrowed, and social benefits such as pensions were substantially increased.

This did not mean that the priorities were reversed. However the measurement is done, all estimates agree that in the USSR a higher proportion of GNP was allocated to investment than in the United States, and that a higher proportion of this investment was allocated to the capital goods industries. This helps to explain why in these years industrial production increased by over 7 per cent a year, more rapidly than in the United States.

Very substantial resources were allocated to defence expenditure, and particularly to investment in and production of armaments. The true figures for all these years have not yet been fully released; in 1950–5, according to archival data, armaments production rose to over twice the level of 1940, increasing by 146 per cent in these five years, as compared with an increase of 85 per cent in industrial production as a whole. With a much smaller GNP than the United States and a technologically less advanced economy, it sought to equal the quantity and quality of United States weapons. At a time of rapid technological advance (missiles, aircraft, nuclear weapons) this placed a continuing strain on Soviet resources. Throughout these years the Soviet Union devoted a higher proportion of GNP to defence than the United States. The eternal problem of maintaining an economically less advanced country as a great military power faced Khrushchev in 1955–64 as it had faced Ivan the Terrible, Peter the Great, Nicholas II and Stalin over four centuries (and still faces Yeltsin today).

The strain of rising defence expenditure was by no means the only major weakness of the Soviet economy in the early 1960s. The rate of growth of agricultural production was far less rapid after 1958: according to official figures, the increase of the three-year average was 45 per cent between 1952–4 and 1957–9, but only 22 per cent between 1957–9 and 1964–6. The grain yields of the Virgin Lands, where climate was subject to great variation, were extremely erratic: 38 million tonnes in 1963, 66 million in 1964, 35 million in 1965, though they continued to make a major contribution to grain output. The slowdown in agricultural growth occurred simultaneously with a falling off in peasant incomes and in the rate of growth of investment in agriculture, which was in turn due to the pressures of the priority given to defence and the capital goods industries.

The economy was also beginning to face other fundamental difficulties. This period saw a great expansion in foreign trade – according to official figures, there was a fivefold increase in real terms between 1950 and 1965 (*Narodnoe khozyaistvo* 1968, pp. 764–8). Two-thirds of this trade was with other Communist countries, largely organised through Comecon (the Council of Mutual Economic Assistance), established in 1949. In the Stalin years this trade was particuarly beneficial to the Soviet Union, which was able to use its political power to enforce favourable prices; but after 1953 Comecon trade was normally carried out in world prices (Nove 1982, pp. 315–16, 351).

Machinery and plant constituted nearly one-third of Soviet imports, and played a significant part in the restoration and modernisation of Soviet industry. But foreign trade was much smaller in relation to national income than in other industrial countries; and Western restrictions prevented the import of the most sophisticated new machinery. In any case, in the Soviet Union as in other industrialising countries, the maturing of industry meant that it was becoming more difficult to advance technologically by acquiring existing technology from abroad. The Soviet Union needed to find the springs of technical innovation from within its own economy. Innovation was particularly needed because labour gradually tended to become more scarce: by the 1960s fewer young workers were available for transfer from the countryside. The economy had increasingly to rely on higher labour productivity and hence on more capital-intensive and/or more efficient production.

By 1965 at least one industrialising economy was proving capable of solving these problems: Japan, whose rate of industrial growth now equalled that of the USSR. But the Soviet Union also showed itself capable of remarkable technical achievements in these years: it launched the first Sputnik in 1957 and the first manned spacecraft in 1961. But could the successes in space research and military technology be generalised? Could advanced technology be widely diffused throughout the economy? We know the answer now; but in 1965 the Soviet Union faced the future with confidence, observed by the capitalist powers with considerable alarm.

# 7

# The Soviet economic system, 1928–1965

The preceding account has shown that the economic system took shape in the early 1930s under the rival influences of ideology and economic necessity. Its major features, established by the mid-1930s, continued more or less unchanged throughout the upheavals of the next half-century. Let us summarise the system as it operated at the time of Stalin's death. Modifications introduced by Khrushchev and others will be considered later in this chapter.

First, as we have seen, agriculture as well as industry was under close state control. State farms (*sovkhozy*) produced a fairly small proportion of total agricultural output. The vast majority of the 25 million peasant households which existed in 1929 were combined into some 250,000 collective farms (*kolkhozy*). In the early 1950s the smaller *kolkhozy* were amalgamated, and the total number was reduced to about 50,000. Most land was pooled, and worked in common. Agricultural machinery was made available to the *kolkhozy* through some 8,000 state-owned Machine-Tractor Stations. Through the system of compulsory deliveries the *kolkhozy* were required to supply a large part of their output to the state collection agencies at low fixed prices.

Secondly, within industry, production and investment were administered through physical controls. Prices were fixed, and materials and capital equipment were distributed to existing factories and new building sites through an allocation system. The state sought through central allocations to give priority to key construction projects and to overcome the bottlenecks in existing industries. The plan set targets for the output of materials, intermediate products and final products. These planning methods resembled both War Communism and the wartime planning controls used in capitalist economies to shift resources to the war effort.

Thirdly, the imposition of the priorities of the state through an economic hierarchy was supplemented by horizontal relations between state enterprises. These horizontal interconnections, involving unplanned and even illegal exchanges and agreements, complemented the rather crude controls of the central plan, and made them workable. Moreover, while the central authorities could always have the final say, a process of bargaining between all levels in the hierarchy, from Politburo to factory department, was crucial to the effectiveness of the plans.

Fourthly, several important market or quasi-market features were incorporated into the planning system in the early 1930s. Restrictions on these arrangements were introduced during the Second World War, but they were resumed before Stalin's death.

(1)  Each peasant household was permitted to work a personal plot, and to possess its own cow and poultry; this private or household sector was responsible for a substantial part of food production.

(2)  After the compulsory deliveries to the state had been completed, each household, and each collective farm as a unit, were permitted to sell their produce on the free market ('collective-farm market') at prices determined by supply and demand. The substantial proportion of their income which they received from these sales on the free market partly compensated the peasants for the low prices they received from the state.

(3)  After the abolition of rationing in 1935, and again following the war in 1947, consumers were free to spend their income, in the state shops or on the free market, on whatever goods were available. In state-owned retail trade, prices were fixed, but the authorities endeavoured – with indifferent success – to balance supply and demand through the use of fiscal measures, particularly the 'turnover tax' (a purchase tax sharply differentiated according to the product).

(4) Most employees were free to change their jobs. Wages were differentiated according to skill and intensity of work, but the existence of the very imperfect labour market meant that wage levels were modified in response to supply and demand. There were major exceptions. The labour of some employees was subject to direct allocation from the centre, especially of course the growing forced-labour sector, but as we have seen restrictions on the movement of labour introduced before and during the war began to be lifted in 1951. Freedom of movement of peasants, however, continued to be severely restricted.

(5) All state enterprises were subject to financial controls through so-called 'economic accounting' (*khozraschet*). Cost reduction targets, set for every ministry and enterprise, were an auxiliary but significant part of the annual plans.

(6) This was then a money economy as well as a physically planned economy. Money flows corresponded to all the physical flows, and some money transactions (for example, wage payments and sales on the free market) were not accompanied by physical controls. The government sought to achieve financial equilibrium by means of a plethora of taxes, credit and cash controls, and currency plans. In practice, however, financial stability was achieved only for a few years before the war (1933–6), before preparations for war and the war itself led to a recrudescence of inflation. The post-war years from the currency reform of 1947 to Stalin's death in 1953 were the great years for financial stability, and in this period retail prices were actually reduced.

The retention of market and quasi-market elements in the economic system led to a shift in the Soviet definition of socialism. 'Socialism' continued to mean a system in which the means of production were owned by the state or by society at large. But from the mid-1930s a moneyless economy based on product exchange was no longer a requirement of socialism; this would only come with the higher stage of 'communism'. Instead socialism as officially redefined involved a money economy, and a socialist form of trade. And the personal plot of the collective-farm household, and the free market associated with it, were regarded as part of this socialist economy; it was for this reason that the 'free market' became known as 'the collective-farm market'. This shift in definition enabled the Soviet authorities to proclaim in 1936 that the USSR had 'already in principle achieved socialism'.

The Soviet economic system was characterised by striking advantages and disadvantages, which manifested themselves to a greater or lesser degree throughout its history (in the long term, some of the short- and medium-term advantages of the system turned out to be disadvantages).

## *Advantages*

First, it succeeded in enforcing the allocation of a very high proportion of GNP to investment in general and to investment in the capital goods and defence industries in particular. This mechanism enabled the successful completion of high-priority crash programmes: the Dnieper dam and the Ural-Kuznetsk iron and steel combine in the 1930s, the nuclear bomb and space programmes after the Second World War – and the achievement of many gold medals in the Olympic Games.

Secondly, central control of investment enabled advanced technology to be diffused rapidly throughout the USSR in certain priority sectors. Project institutes for such industries as iron and steel were able to plan technological advance for a whole industry on a national scale.

Thirdly, important economies of scale were achieved through the standardisation of products.

Fourthly, the production drive successfully induced managers and workers to exert great efforts to fulfil the plans.

## *Disadvantages*

First, the cost of concentrating resources on the capital goods industries and defence was very high. Its consequences, long-term as well as short-term, for agriculture have already been described. It should also be noted that the death of large numbers of horses and other draught-animals during collectivisation had the unintended consequence that the state was forced to reallocate resources to the agricultural machinery industry, and hence to the high-grade steel industry.

Secondly, when politicians or central planners made a wrong technological choice the cost was proportionately heavy, because the policy was carried out on a national scale. Thus, for example, in the 1940s there was overinvestment in the coal industry and underinvestment in oil and chemicals.

Thirdly, the centralised system also proved inherently clumsy in its effects at the point of production. If success indicators set by the planners were very detailed, initiative and innovation at factory level were prevented. But if they were imprecise, factories produced what it was easier to produce, rather than what was wanted. Control of quality through centrally determined indicators also proved very difficult.

Fourthly, the repressed inflation and sellers' market which was an integral part of the system reinforced these difficulties. At the same time the sellers' market led each industrial ministry or sub-ministry to seek to become a self-contained 'empire', carrying out wasteful backward integration in order to control its supplies. If advertising and inflated sales organisations are a costly feature of modern capitalism, inflated supply organisations were a high cost of administrative planning.

By the end of the 1930s it was already becoming apparent that the system which had managed to bring about technological revolution and economic growth from above was incapable, without drastic reform, of encouraging technological innovation from below. This and other deficiencies became even more obvious in Khrushchev's time; and from 1954 onwards major efforts, increasingly desperate, were made to reform the system.

In 1954–6 the central authorities undertook 'step-by-step' de-centralisation. They sought to shed some of their powers by reducing the number of planning indicators set by the government. The intention was that each ministry responsible for a particular industry would devolve some of its authority to its departments and to the individual state firms. The reform was on the whole unsuccessful. Ministries used their increased authority to bind their 'empires' more closely together.

In 1957 Khrushchev embarked on his drastic scheme for the regionalisation of industry. Industrial ministries were abolished, and replaced by regional economic councils responsible for all the factories in the region. What eventually emerged was a mixture of area-by-area and industry-by-industry control. But economic administration was so complicated that the old ministries were restored in 1965, less than a year after Khrushchev's fall.

In 1958 the agricultural machinery managed by the state-owned Machine-Tractor Stations was sold to the *kolkhozy*, so that they now owned their own tractors, combine harvesters and other major items of equipment as well as agricultural implements. The intention was to encourage *kolkhozy* to act as autonomous economic units. But the reform was hasty and poorly thought out; and no change was made in the structure of agricultural trade and prices. It compounded the difficulties of agriculture.

These reforms were all conducted within the framework of the physical planning system, and involved little or no extension of the market sector of the economy. The growth of the market sector was limited by restrictions placed on the collective farmers' personal plots and on the *kolkhoz* market. Much discussion took place about the possibility of replacing administrative planning by some form of 'market socialism', in which state firms would take their decisions not as a result of plans imposed from above but in response to signals from a state-controlled but relatively free market – a kind of modern NEP. But the political leaders believed that market socialism would disrupt the Soviet political system, and refused to contemplate any such reform (their belief seemed to be confirmed a few years after Khrushchev's fall by the Czechoslovak upheaval in 1968). After all, they argued, the economy is doing pretty well by international standards, and the central planning system has enabled the Soviet Union to become one of the two world superpowers. 'We will bury you', Mr Khrushchev told the capitalist world.

# 8
# Soviet industrialisation in perspective

By 1965 the Soviet economic system, at great human cost, had negotiated the first stages of the industrialisation of a developing country; and in the international arena the Soviet Union had emerged after the Second World War as one of the world's two superpowers. Industrialisation had brought about a major social transformation. In 1965, 33 million people were employed in industry and construction, as compared with 5 million in 1928; and the total number of graduates was now nearly 5 million, over twenty times as many as the 233,000 in 1928.

But the Soviet system had not been designed merely as an instrument for industrialisation. It had also been intended, ever since 1917, to provide a blueprint or starting point for the establishment of a planned socialist economic order throughout the world. To maintain this programme, the Soviet system of the 1960s had to find means of coping with the problems of economic growth and technical change in a more advanced industrial society.

The history of the quarter of a century between 1965 and the collapse of the Soviet Union in 1991 was the story of its failure to solve these problems. In the 1970s and 1980s the Soviet Union failed to reduce the technological gap between its industry and that of the major Western countries. From the mid-1970s onwards, the growth of agricultural production barely kept pace with the growth of population. As early as the mid-1970s, the rate of economic growth had fallen so far that, for the first time since the mid-1920s, GNP was increasing less rapidly than in the United States – and much more slowly than in several newly industrialised countries.

The inherent weaknesses of the Soviet economic system, which we have considered in these pages, certainly played an important role in the failure to reform the system, and in the ultimate collapse of Soviet communism. We have seen that ever since 1930 the Soviet economy, in spite of its industrial dynamism, suffered from inherent defects as consequences of the sellers' market and the strong central control over industry. In industry and trade, quality and the needs of the consumer were neglected. Initiative was fettered and risk was discouraged; and above all the centralised system, while often successfully launching new technological policies from above, inhibited the development of new production and new technology by factories and enterprises. And ever since 1928 the Soviet economy was haunted and partly paralysed by its inability to secure agricultural advance.

But in the last decades of communism several new factors on the world scene exacerbated the problems of the Soviet system. It was in the post-war years, and particularly in the 1970s and 1980s, that the capitalist world demonstrated its ability to initiate and launch new technological revolutions: the capitalist system challenged by Soviet communism was profoundly different from capitalism in the 1930s. Moreover, the Western alliance led by the United States, reinforced by the new technology, embarked in the 1970s on the comprehensive modernisation of its armed forces. The Soviet leaders under Brezhnev, like their Tsarist predecessors, took the perhaps fatal decision to embark on a huge and unsuccessful effort to secure military superiority, placing an immense strain on the relatively less advanced Soviet economy. And at the heart of the economic difficulties of the 1970s and 1980s was the inability of the Soviet leadership under both Brezhnev and Gorbachev to reform the economic system. The 1965 economic reform improved industrial administration, and led to a temporary improvement in economic growth. But it was ultimately unsuccessful, as were the subsequent attempts at reform, including the sweeping changes introduced by Gorbachev after 1985. How far was this failure due to the inherent impossibility of transforming state socialism into a kind of market socialism, how far was it a defect of the talents and imagination of the political leaders and their advisers – or of the ruling élite as a whole?

To explain the collapse of the Soviet economy and the Soviet system, like other major economic changes elsewhere in the world, we need to take into account not only economic but also political and social factors. The Soviet Union was a one-party state, and in the course of its development, contrary to the intentions of its founders, a new ruling élite, often characterised as a new ruling class, emerged into a dominant position. The absence of other political parties – and even of serious political discussion within the single party – hindered the emergence of innovative ideas and encouraged the stagnation of the élite. A rigid censorship greatly restricted the free flow of ideas within the Soviet Union and between the Soviet Union and the West. And, ever since the Civil War, the secret police – known variously as the OGPU, the NKVD and the KGB – had acquired vast powers, which, although moderated after the death of Stalin, were exercised against every kind of dissent.

Although Soviet communism has come to an abrupt end, Soviet industrialisation has exerted a profound and lasting influence on world economic development. The inhumanities and social inequalities of the Stalinist version of socialism antagonised both the élites and the ordinary people in the Western democracies. But the first stage of Soviet industrial advance took place in the 1930s, the years of the world economic crisis. The ability of the Soviet state to produce a dynamic economic system exercised a profound influence on Western economic thinking, and was undoubtedly a factor in the emergence of the mixture of state and private control and ownership that was characteristic of most Western industrial countries in the first thirty years or so after the Second World War.

Soviet success in transforming a largely peasant country into an industrial superpower within a few decades profoundly influenced the outlook and psychology of the four-fifths of the world which was not yet industrialised. The efforts of some Third World countries to emulate the Soviet model of state-managed economic development ended in failure. But in spite of the shift of the Third World towards capitalism in recent decades, Soviet industrialisation remained a yardstick against which the economic success or failure of ex-colonial countries tended to be measured. In the economic history of the world, Soviet industrialisation was an important stage in the spreading of the economic and social

transformation which began in England in the eighteenth century
to the thousands of millions of peasants who lived on the edge of
starvation.

Table 10 *Gross national product by sector of origin, 1928–65*

| | (Billion rubles at 1937 prices) | | | | | | | | |
|---|---|---|---|---|---|---|---|---|---|
| | 1928 | 1932 | 1937 | 1940 | 1945 | 1946 | 1950 | 1955 | 1960 | 1965 |
| Agriculture | 58.0 | 41.9 | 63.0 | 69.9 | 47.1 | 51.7 | 74.0 | 88.1 | 115.2 | 133 |
| Industry | 24.2 | 37.6 | 65.4 | 77.8 | 53.8 | 54.5 | 101.6 | 165.0 | 244.8 | 336 |
| Other | 41.5 | 56.2 | 83.9 | 102.8 | 98.1 | 92.2 | 128.7 | 188.5 | 267.0 | (325) |
| Total | 123.7 | 135.7 | 212.3 | 250.5 | 199.0 | 198.4 | 304.3 | 441.6 | 627.0 | 794 |

*Source:* Estimated from Moorsteen and Powell 1966, pp. 620–38; data for
1965 are approximations using growth rates for agriculture, industry and
total GNP estimated by the CIA in *Measures* 1990, table A-1.

Table 11 *Non-agricultural employment by sector of the economy,*
        *1928–65*

| | (Thousands) | | | | | |
|---|---|---|---|---|---|---|
| | 1928 | 1932 | 1940 | 1945 | 1950 | 1965 |
| Industry | 4,339 | 9,374 | 13,079 | 10,665 | 15,317 | 27,056 |
| Building | 818 | 2,458 | 1,993 | 1,774 | 3,278 | 5,617 |
| Transport and communications | 1,397 | 2,370 | 4,009 | 3,552 | 4,659 | 8,259 |
| Trade | 606 | 2,223 | 3,351 | 2,445 | 3,360 | 6,009 |
| Education, science, culture, art | 847 | 1,512 | 3,213 | 2,786 | 4,214 | 8,760 |
| Health | 399 | 669 | 1,512 | 1,419 | 2,051 | 4,277 |
| Administration, etc. | 1,010 | 1,650 | 1,837 | 1,645 | 1,831 | 1,460 |
| Domestic help and day labour | 809 | 342 | – | – | – | – |
| Other | 293 | 922 | 1,949 | 1,350 | 1,829 | 5,912 |
| Total | 10,518 | 21,520 | 30,943 | 25,636 | 36,539 | 67,350 |

*Note:* See first source for the coverage of this table. The 1965 data are not
entirely consistent with those for earlier years; in particular, employment
in 'art', including museums, etc., is omitted from the 1965 figure for
'Education', etc. It amounted to 315,000 in 1960 and 380,000 in 1966.
*Source:* Davies, Harrison and Wheatcroft 1994, pp. 280–1; *Trud* 1968, pp.
24–5 and 1988, pp. 30–1.

# Further reading

The best general account of Soviet economic history is Nove 1982, which covers the whole epoch dealt with in this book. Davies, Harrison and Wheatcroft 1994 considers each major branch of the economy for the years from 1914 to 1941. Zaleski 1971 and 1980 provide systematic comparisons of plan and performance for the years 1928 to 1953.

## Main sources on each period

*Tsarist economy.* Falkus 1972 is an excellent survey of the rise of industry from Peter the Great to the First World War. For the immediate pre-war years, Gatrell 1986 is the fullest account; both this book and Crisp 1976 thoughtfully discuss the major controversies. For national income, see the thorough analysis in Gregory 1982.

*First World War.* For war preparations, see Gatrell 1994a; for the economy as a whole, see Gatrell 1994b; for industry, see Siegelbaum 1983.

*War Communism.* The classic brief accounts are in Dobb 1928 and 1948 and Baykov 1948. Economic policy is dealt with in detail in Carr 1952. A thorough survey using more recent findings is Malle 1985. For the important question of food policy, see Lih 1990.

*New Economic Policy.* Dobb 1928 and 1948 have much valuable material. The fullest accounts are in Carr 1952, Carr 1958 and Carr and Davies 1969. For a thorough comparison of the late Tsarist economy and NEP, see Davies 1990, to which historians with different viewpoints about NEP contribute. For recent Soviet discussions of NEP, see Davies 1989c and 1997. Danilov 1988 is an examination of agriculture in the 1920s by the foremost Russian specialist. For a pioneering account of the textile industry during NEP, see Ward 1990.

*The pre-war industrialisation drive, 1928–41.*    The breakdown of NEP and the emergence of the Stalinist central planning system are discussed from different viewpoints in Millar 1974, Davies 1980 and 1989b, and Hunter and Szyrmer 1992. Harrison 1980 sums up the controversy.

Problems of Soviet statistics in the Stalin period are discussed in Wheatcroft and Davies 1994a.

For economic policy see, as well as the invaluable Zaleski 1980, Rees 1997, which includes the recent archive-based findings of young Russian as well as Western historians, and Davies 1996.

For particular sectors of the economy see the various chapters in Davies, Harrison and Wheatcroft 1994; for industry and agriculture, the highly critical and well-informed Jasny 1949 and 1961; for science and industry, Lewis 1979; for railways, Hunter 1957 and Westwood 1982; for foreign trade, Dohan and Hewett 1973. For a case study of the new iron and steel complex at Magnitogorsk, see Kotkin 1995 and the eye-witness account in Scott 1971.

*Second World War.*    Barber and Harrison 1991 is an outstanding general introduction. For more detail, consult Harrison 1985 and Harrison 1996; the latter is based on material recently released from Russian archives. Food policy is discussed in Moskoff 1990. For a comparison of the Russian/Soviet economies in the two world wars, see Gatrell and Harrison 1993.

*Post-war recovery and expansion.*    No separate monographs are available on the economic history of this period, but much valuable information will be found in Nove 1982, Zaleski 1980, Jasny 1961 (for industry), Strauss 1969 (for agriculture) and Filtzer 1993 (for a critical view of the Khrushchev period).

# References

The references below are restricted to works in English, with the exception of a few statistical handbooks in Russian. References to important material in Russian may be found in Nove 1982, Davies 1990, and Davies, Harrison and Wheatcroft 1994.

Bacon, E. 1994, *The Gulag at War: The Soviet Forced Labour System in the Light of the Archives*, London and Basingstoke.

Bailes, K. E. 1978, *Technology and Society under Lenin and Stalin: Origins of the Soviet Technical Intelligentsia, 1917–1941*, Princeton, N.J.

Barber, J. 1978, 'The Composition of the Soviet Working Class, 1928–1941', Discussion Paper, SIPS no. 16, CREES, University of Birmingham.

1981, *Soviet Historians in Crisis, 1928–1932*, London and Basingstoke.

Barber, J. and Davies, R.W. 1994, 'Employment and Industrial Labour', in Davies, Harrison and Wheatcroft (eds.), pp. 81–105.

Barber, J. and Harrison, M. 1991, *The Soviet Home Front, 1941–1945: a Social and Economic History of the USSR in World War II* , London.

Barker, G. R. no date [1955], *Some Problems of Incentives and Labour Productivity in Soviet Industry*, Oxford.

Barnett, V. 1995, 'A Long Wave Goodbye: Kondrat'ev and the Conjuncture Institute, 1920–28', *Europe–Asia Studies*, 47: 413–41.

Baykov, A. 1948, *The Development of the Soviet Economic System*, Cambridge.

1954, 'The Economic Development of Russia', *Economic History Review* (2nd series), 7: 137–49.

Bergson, A. 1961, *The Real National Income of Soviet Russia since 1928*, Cambridge, Mass.

Bergson A. and Kuznets, S. 1963 (eds.), *Economic Trends in the Soviet Union*, Cambridge, Mass.

Carr, E. H. 1952, *The Bolshevik Revolution, 1917–1923*, vol. 2, London.

1958, *Socialism in One Country, 1924–1926*, vol. 1, London.

1967, 'Some Random Reflections on Soviet Industrialization', in Feinstein (ed.), pp. 271–84.

1978, *The Russian Revolution from Lenin to Stalin*, London and Basingstoke.

Carr, E. H. and Davies, R. W. 1969, *Foundations of a Planned Economy, 1926–1929*, vol. 1, London.

Channon, J. 1987, 'Tsarist Landowners after the Revolution: Former Pomeshchiki in Rural Russia during NEP', *Soviet Studies*, 34: 575–98.

1992, 'The Landowners', in Service (ed.), pp. 120–46.

Cherniavsky, M. 1970 (ed.), *The Structure of Russian History: Interpretative Essays*, New York.

Clark, C. 1939, *A Critique of Soviet Statistics*, London.

2nd edn 1951, 3rd edn 1957, *Conditions of Economic Progress*, London.

Clarke, R. A. 1972, *Soviet Economic Facts, 1917–70*, London and Basingstoke.

Cohen, S. F. 1974, *Bukharin and the Bolshevik Revolution: A Political Biography, 1888–1938*, London.

Conquest, R. 1968, *The Great Terror: Stalin's Purge of the Thirties*, London.

1986, *The Harvest of Sorrow: Soviet Collectivisation and the Terror Famine*, London.

Cooper, J. M. and Lewis, R. A. 1990, 'Research and Technology', in Davies (ed.), pp. 189–211.

Crisp, O. 1976, *Studies in the Russian Economy Before 1914*, London.

1978, 'Labour and Industrialization in Russia', in Mathias and Postan (eds.), pp. 308–415, 573–80.

Danilov, V. P. 1988, *Rural Russia under the New Regime*, London and Bloomington, Ind.

Davies, R.W. 1955/6, 'Economic Incentives – I', *Soviet Studies*, 7: 451–4.

1958, *The Development of the Soviet Budgetary System* , Cambridge.

1969/70, 'A Note on Grain Statistics', *Soviet Studies*, 21: 314–29.

1980, *The Socialist Offensive: The Collectivisation of Soviet Agriculture, 1929–1930*, London.

1989a, 'Economic and Social Policy in the USSR, 1917–41', in Mathias and Pollard (eds.), pp. 984–1047, 1199–203.

1989b, *The Soviet Economy in Turmoil, 1929–1930*, London and Basingstoke.

1989c, *Soviet History in the Gorbachev Revolution*, London and Basingstoke.

Davies, R. W. 1990 (ed.), *From Tsarism to the New Economic Policy: Continuity and Change in the Economy of the USSR*, London and Basingstoke.

1996, *Crisis and Progress in the Soviet Economy, 1931–1933*, London and Basingstoke.

1997, *Soviet History in the Yeltsin Era*, London and Basingstoke.

Davies, R. W., Harrison, M. and Wheatcroft, S. G. 1994 (eds.), *The Economic Transformation of the Soviet Union, 1913–1945*, Cambridge.

Davis, C. M., 'Russian Industrial Policy and Performance, 1900–2000', in Foreman-Peck, Hannah and Federico (eds.) (in preparation).

Dobb, M. H. 1928, *Russian Economic Development since the Revolution*, London.

1948, *Soviet Economic Development since 1917*, London.

Dohan, M. R. 1976, 'The Economic Origins of Soviet Autarky, 1927/28–1934', *Slavic Review*, 35: 603–35.

1990, 'Foreign Trade', in Davies (ed.), pp. 212–33.

Dohan, M. R. and Hewett, E. 1973, *Two Studies in Soviet Terms of Trade, 1918–1970*, Bloomington, Ind.

Erlich, A. 1960, *The Soviet Industrialization Debate*, Cambridge, Mass.

Falkus, M. E. 1972, *The Industrialisation of Russia, 1700–1914*, London.

Feinstein, C. H. 1967 (ed.), *Socialism, Capitalism and Economic Growth: Essays Presented to Maurice Dobb*, Cambridge.

Figes, O. 1989, *Peasant Russia, Civil War: The Volga Countryside in Revolution, 1917–1921*, Oxford.

Filtzer, D. 1993, *The Khrushchev Era: De-Stalinisation and the Limits of Reform in the USSR, 1953–1964*, London and Basingstoke.

Fitzpatrick, S. 1979, *Education and Social Mobility in the Soviet Union, 1921–1934*, Cambridge.

1994, *Stalin's Peasants: Resistance and Survival in the Russian Village after Collectivization*, Oxford.

Fitzpatrick, S. and Viola, L. 1987, *A Researcher's Guide to Sources on Soviet Social History in the 1930s*, Armonk, N.Y.

Foreman-Peck, J., Hannah, L. and Federico, G. (eds.), *A Century of European Industrial Policy* (in preparation).

Gatrell, P. 1982, 'Industrial Expansion in Tsarist Russia,1908–1914', *Economic History Review* (2nd series), 35: 99–110.

1986, *The Tsarist Economy, 1850–1917*, London.

1994a, *Government, Industry and Rearmament in Russia, 1900–1914*, Cambridge.

1994b, 'The First World War and War Communism, 1914–1920', in Davies, Harrison and Wheatcroft (eds.), pp. 216–37.

Gatrell, P. and Davies, R. W. 1990, 'The Industrial Economy', in Davies (ed.), pp. 127–59.

Gatrell, P. and Harrison, M. 1993, 'The Russian and Soviet Economies in Two World Wars: A Comparative View', *Economic History Review* (2nd series), 46: 425–52.

Gerschenkron A. 1965, *Economic Backwardness in Historical Perspective: a Book of Essays*, New York.

Geyer, D. 1987, *Russian Imperialism: The Interaction of Domestic and Foreign Policy, 1860–1914*, London.

Goldman, M. I. 1967, *Soviet Foreign Aid*, New York.

Gregory, P. R. 1982, *Russian National Income, 1885–1913*, Cambridge.

1983, 'The Russian Agrarian Crisis Revisited', in Stuart (ed.), pp. 21–6.

1990, 'National Income', in Davies (ed.), pp. 237–47.

1994, *Before Command: An Economic History of Russia from Emancipation to the First Five-Year Plan*, Princeton, N.J.

1996, 'Searching for Consistency in Historical Data: Alternate Estimates of Russia's Industrial Production, 1887 to 1913', unpublished paper, University of Houston, Texas.

Haimson, L. 1970, 'The Problem of Social Stability in Urban Russia, 1905–1917', in Cherniavsky (ed.), pp. 341–80.

1988, 'The Problem of Social Identities in Early Twentieth Century Russia', *Slavic Review*, 47: 512–17.

Harrison, M. 1980, 'Why Did NEP Fail?', *Economics of Planning*, 16: 57–67.

1985, *Soviet Planning in Peace and War, 1938–1945*, Cambridge.

1990a, 'The Peasantry and Industrialisation', in Davies (ed.), pp. 104–24.

1990b, 'Stalinist Industrialisation and the Test of War', *History Workshop Journal*, no. 29, pp. 65–84.

1993, 'Soviet Economic Growth Since 1928: The Alternative Statistics of G. I. Khanin', *Europe–Asia Studies*, 45: 141–67.

1994a, 'National Income', in Davies, Harrison and Wheatcroft (eds.), pp. 38–56.

1994b, 'The Second World War', in Davies, Harrison and Wheatcroft (eds.), pp. 238–67.

1996, *Accounting for War: Soviet Production, Employment and the Defence Burden, 1940–1945*, Cambridge.

Harrison, M. and Davies, R. W. 1997, 'The Soviet Military-Economic Effort in the Second Five-Year Plan (1933–37)', *Europe–Asia Studies*, 49: 369–406.

Hoffman, D. L. 1994, *Peasant Metropolis: Social Identities in Moscow, 1929–1941*, Ithaca, N.Y.

Hunter, H. 1957, *Soviet Transportation Policy*, Cambridge, Mass.

Hunter, H. and Szyrmer, J. M. 1992, *Faulty Foundations: Soviet Economic Policies, 1928–1940*, Princeton, N.J.

Ilič, M. 1996, 'Women Workers in the Soviet Mining Industry: A Case-study of Labour Protection', *Europe–Asia Studies*, 48: 1387–1402.

Jasny, N. 1949, *The Socialized Agriculture of the USSR: Plans and Performance*, Stanford, Calif.

1961, *Soviet Industrialization, 1928–1952*, Chicago.

1962, *Essays on the Soviet Economy*, New York.

1972, *Soviet Economists of the Twenties: Names to be Remembered*, Cambridge.

Kahan, A. 1967, 'Government Policies and the Industrialization of Russia', *Journal of Economic History*, 27: 460–77.

Karcz, J. F. 1966/7, 'Thoughts on the Grain Problem', *Soviet Studies*, 18: 394–434.

1970/1, 'Back on the Grain Front', *Soviet Studies*, 22: 262–94.

Kaufman, A. 1962, *Small-scale Industry in the Soviet Union*, Occasional Paper 80, National Bureau of Economic Research, New York.

Kenez, P. 1977, *Civil War in South Russia, 1919–1920*, Berkeley and London.

Kotkin, S. 1995, *Magnetic Mountain: Stalinism as a Civilization*, Berkeley, Calif., Los Angeles and London.

*Kul'turnoe stroitel'stvo SSSR: statisticheskii sbornik*, 1956, Moscow.

Lampert, N. 1979, *The Technical Intelligentsia and the Soviet State: A Study of Soviet Managers and Technologists, 1928–1935*, London.

Lenin, V. I. 1936–8, *Selected Works*, 12 vols. London.

Lewis, R. A. 1979, *Science and Industrialisation in the USSR*, London and Basingstoke.

1994a, 'Foreign Economic Relations', in Davies, Harrison and Wheatcroft (eds.), pp. 198–215.

1994b, 'Technology and the Transformation of the Soviet Economy', in Davies, Harrison and Wheatcroft (eds.), pp. 182–97.

Lieven, D. C. B. 1983, *Russia and the Origins of the First World War*, London.

Lih, L. T. 1986, 'Bolshevik *Razverstka* and War Communism', *Slavic Review*, 45: 673–88.

1990, *Bread and Authority in Russia, 1914–1921*, Berkeley, Calif., and Los Angeles.

Lorimer, F. 1946, *The Population of the Soviet Union: History and Prospects*, Geneva.

Malafeev, A. N. 1964, *Istoriya tsenoobrazovaniya v SSSR (1917–1963gg.)*, Moscow.

Malle, S. 1985, *The Economic Organisation of War Communism, 1918–1921*, Cambridge.

Mathias, P. and Pollard, S. 1989 (eds.), *Cambridge Economic History of Europe*, vol. VIII, Cambridge.

Mathias, P. and Postan, M. M. 1978 (eds.), *Cambridge Economic History of Europe*, vol. VII, part 2, Cambridge.

McKay, J. P. 1970, *Pioneers for Profit. Foreign Entrepreneurship and Russian Industrialisation, 1885–1913*, Chicago and London.

*Measures of Soviet Gross National Product in 1982 Prices: A Study Prepared for the Use of the Joint Economic Committee, Congress of the United States*, 1990, Washington, D.C.

Millar, J. 1974, 'Mass Collectivization and the Contribution of Soviet Agriculture to the First Five-Year Plan: A Review Article', *Slavic Review*, 33: 750–66.

Millar, J. and Nove, A. 1976, 'A Debate on Collectivisation', *Problems of Communism*, 25 (July–August): 49–62.

Miller, J. 1952/3, 'A Contrast in Types of Party Leadership', *Soviet Studies*, 4: 447–68.

Moorsteen R. and Powell, R. P. 1966, *The Soviet Capital Stock, 1928–1962*, Homewood, Ill.

Moskoff, W. 1990, *The Bread of Affliction: The Food Supply in the USSR during World War II*, Cambridge.

*Narodnoe khozyaistvo SSSR v 1958g.: statisticheskii ezhegodnik*, 1959, Moscow.

*Narodnoe khozyaistvo SSSR v 1967g.: statisticheskii ezhegodnik*, 1968, Moscow.

Nove, A. 1982, *An Economic History of the USSR*, revised edn (1st edn, 1969) London and Harmondsworth.

    1990, 'How Many Victims in the 1930s?', *Soviet Studies*, 42: 369–73, 811–14.

Nutter, G.W. 1962, *Growth of Industrial Production in the Soviet Union*, Princeton, N.J.

Preobrazhensky, E. A. 1965, *The New Economics*, Oxford.

Rees, A. 1997 (ed.), *Decision-Making in the Stalinist Command Economy 1932–37*, London and Basingstoke.

Scott, J. 1971 (originally published 1942), *Behind the Urals: An American Worker in Russia's City of Steel*, New York.

*Sel'skoe khozyaistvo SSSR: statisticheskii sbornik*, 1960, Moscow.

*Sel'skoe khozyaistvo SSSR: statisticheskii sbornik*, 1971, Moscow.

Service, R. 1992 (ed.), *Society and Politics in the Russian Revolution*, London and Basingstoke.

Seton-Watson, H. 1952, *The Decline of Imperial Russia*, London.

Shanin, T. 1972, *The Awkward Class: Political Sociology of Peasantry in a Developing Society: Russia, 1910–1925*, Oxford.

    1985, *Russia as a 'Developing Society'*, London.

Siegelbaum, L. 1983, *The Politics of Industrial Mobilization in Russia, 1914–1917: A Study of the War Industries Committees* , London.

    1988, *Stakhanovism and the Politics of Productivity in the USSR, 1935–1941*, Cambridge.

Solomon, S. G. 1977, *The Soviet Agrarian Debate: A Controversy in Social Science, 1923–1929*, Boulder, Colo.

Spulber, N. 1964, *Foundations of a Soviet Strategy for Economic Growth*, Bloomington, Ind.

Strauss, E. 1969, *Soviet Agriculture in Perspective*, London.

Stuart, R. C. 1983 (ed.), *The Soviet Rural Economy*, Totowa, N.J.

Sutton, A. C. 1968, *Western Technology and Soviet Economic Development, 1917–1930*, Stanford.

Swaniewicz, S. 1965, *Forced Labour and Economic Development: An Enquiry into the Experience of Soviet Industrialization*, Oxford.

Szamuely, L. 1974, *First Models of the Socialist Economic Systems: Principles and Theories*, Budapest.

*Trud v SSSR: statisticheskii spravochnik*, 1968 and 1988, Moscow.

Tucker, R. C. 1974, *Stalin as Revolutionary, 1879–1929: A Study in History and Personality*, New York.

von Laue, T. H. 1963, *Sergei Witte and the Industrialization of Russia*, New York.

1966, *Why Lenin ? Why Stalin ? A Reappraisal of the Russian Revolution, 1900–30*, London.

Ward, C. 1990, *Russia's Cotton Workers and the New Economic Policy: Shop-floor Culture and State Policy*, Cambridge.

Westwood, J. N. 1982, *Soviet Locomotive Technology During Industrialisation, 1928–1952*, London and Basingstoke.

Wheatcroft, S. G. 1984, 'Doctors and the Revolution in Russia', *Bulletin of the Society of the Social History of Medicine*, no. 34: 19–24.

1990, 'Agriculture', in Davies (ed.), pp. 79–103.

1996, 'The Scale and Nature of German and Soviet Repression and Mass Killings, 1930–45', *Europe–Asia Studies*, 48: 1319–55.

Wheatcroft, S. G. and Davies, R. W. 1985 (eds.), *Materials for a Balance of the Soviet National Economy, 1928–1930*, Cambridge.

Wheatcroft, S. G. and Davies, R. W. 1994a, 'The Crooked Mirror of Soviet Statistics', in Davies, Harrison and Wheatcroft (eds.), pp. 24–37.

1994b, 'Population', in Davies, Harrison and Wheatcroft (eds.), pp. 57–80.

1994c, 'Agriculture', in Davies, Harrison and Wheatcroft (eds.), pp. 106–30.

Wheatcroft, S. G., Davies, R. W. and Cooper, J. M. 1986, 'Soviet Industrialization Reconsidered: Some Preliminary Conclusions About Soviet Economic Development Between 1926 and 1941', *Economic History Review* (2nd series), 39: 264–94.

Zaleski, E. 1971, *Planning for Economic Growth in the Soviet Union, 1918–1932*, Chapel Hill, N.C.

1980, *Stalinist Planning for Economic Growth, 1933–1952*, London and Basingstoke.

Zima, V. F. 1993, 'Golod v Rossii 1946–1947 godov', *Otechestvennaya istoriya*, 1: 35–52.

# Index

administrative economy, 4, 67
agricultural production
  1930s, 57
  first five-year plan, 45
  NEP, 25, 27
  post-war, 64, 65, 68, 69, 71, 79
  pre-revolutionary, 9, 10, 13
  Second World War, 60, 61
  *see also* harvest; livestock
agriculture, 73, 77
  1930s, 43, 53, 54, 57
  NEP, 25, 26, 33
  personal plots, 48, 53, 74, 76, 78
  post-war, 66, 69, 78
  pre-revolutionary, 10, 14, 15
  Second World War, 62
  War Communism, 19
  *see also* collectivisation; cotton;
    grain; Stolypin reforms; Virgin
    Lands
aircraft, 44, 63, 71
Alexander II, 6
armaments, 38, 63, 76
  production, 15, 41, 44, 45, 55, 59,
    61, 62, 64, 65, 66, 71
armed forces, 60, 62, 80
artisan industry, 9, 10, 23, 24, 26
atom bomb, *see* nuclear bomb
Austria, 55

Baku, 44
Baltic states, 23
banks, 21, 24
Barsov, A. A., 57
barter, 4, 19, 23, 52; *see also* trade
Baykov, A., 7
Bazarov, V. A., 33

Bergson, A., 39, 40, 41, 42
birth deficit, 2
Bolsheviks, 12, 17, 20, 21, 32, 33
boom
  1890s, 7, 8, 11
  1908–13, 10
Bovykin, V. I., 12
Brezhnev, L., 80
Britain, 1, 3, 4, 6, 9, 61
budget, 7, 11, 54, 56
Bukharin, N., 34, 35, 36

camps, *see* forced labour
Canada, 1
capital accumulation, 26
capital construction, 34, 50, 52, 65;
    *see also* investment
capital goods industries, 76
  1930s, 5, 43, 44, 45, 51
  NEP, 32
  post-war, 66, 68, 69, 71
  pre-revolutionary, 7, 8, 9, 10
Carr, E. H., 35
cartels, *see* syndicates
censorship, 25, 81
census of population
  1926, 38, 46, 47, 50
  1939, 38, 46, 47, 50
  1959, 38, 64
Central Asia, 1, 45
Central Black-Earth region, 14
central planning, 4, 19
Chayanov, A. V., 33
Chechens, 49, 63
chemical industry, 59, 69, 77
China, 2
Civil War, 2, 18, 21, 34, 63, 64

coal, 7, 9, 66, 77
Cohen, S., 36
collective farms (*kolkhozy*), 47, 48,
    53, 58, 73, 78
collective-farm market, *see* market(s)
collectivisation, 36, 47, 48, 51, 52,
    53, 54, 57, 58, 77
combine harvesters, 58, 67, 78
Comecon, 72
communism, 17, 75
Communist Party, 13, 26, 30, 32
Communist Party Congress
    (X, 1921), 23
    (XVI, 1930), 51
Conquest, R., 49
consumer goods industries
    1930s, 5, 39, 45, 57–8
    post-war, 66, 68, 69
    pre-revolutionary, 9, 10, 15
    War Communism, 18, 59
consumption, 40, 45, 46, 52
cotton, 29, 45, 48, 57, 66, 67; *see also*
    textile industries
Crisp, O., 7, 13
currency, 18, 19, 20, 25, 52, 54; *see*
    *also* money; ruble
currency reform,
    1924, 24
    1947, 75
Czechoslovakia, 55, 78

deaths,
    crude rate, 70
    excess, 2, 50, 63
    *see also* infant mortality; population
decentralisation, 77
defence, 11, 40, 59, 61, 62, 76
defence expenditure, 11, 39, 55, 71
defence industry, *see* armaments
dekulakisation, 48, 51, 53; *see also*
    collectivisation
Denikin, General A. I., 20
depression (1899–1902), 8, 9
Dnieper dam, 44, 59, 76
Dobb, M., 19, 32
Donbass, 44
Duma, 8

economic accounting, *see khozraschet*
education, 46, 67, 68, 70
    higher education, 46, 67, 70

electrical engineering, 11
electric power stations, 44, 66
Emancipation Act (1861), 6, 9
emergency measures, 34, 51
employment, 43, 57, 68, 82
    in agriculture, 10, 62
    in construction, 38, 79
    in industry, 6, 9, 16, 38, 52, 79
engineering industry, 7, 9, 15, 44,
    66; *see also* machine-building
    industry
equality, 25, 26
Erlich, A., 32, 33
exile, 48, 50, 54; *see also* forced
    labour
exports, 25, 27; *see also* foreign trade

famine, 2
    1921–2, 22, 25, 64
    1933, 2, 45, 48, 50, 54
    1947, 64
Far East, 50
Finland, 23
First World War, *see* World War
five-year plan
    first (1928–32), 44, 45, 46, 51, 54
    second (1933–7), 54
    fourth (1946–50), 65
flax, 29, 48, 67
food, 10, 23, 27, 39, 40, 45, 54, 63,
    74
    requisitioning, 21
    supply, 16, 20, 30, 52, 57
footwear, 66
forced labour, 48–50, 62, 68, 70, 75
    conditions, 50
foreign capital, 10, 11, 12, 13
foreign loans, 7
foreign technology, 43–4
foreign trade, 13, 21, 23, 25, 27, 44,
    71–2; *see also* exports; imports
fourth five-year plan, *see* five-year
    plan
France, 1, 9
fuel, 9, 23, 44, 59

Germany, 1, 3, 9, 15, 16, 20, 31, 55,
    59, 65
Gerschenkron, A., 3, 10, 11, 13, 15,
    35
Geyer, D., 15

Gindin, I. F., 12, 13
*glasnost'*, 41
gold, 50
gold standard, 7, 11
Gorbachev, M. S., 4, 12, 35, 80
Gorinov, M. M., 36
grain, 48, 57, 60
  exports, 15
  marketing of, 27, 29
  output, 14, 15, 23, 41, 66, 69, 71
  prices, *see* prices
  requisitioning, 18, 20, 23
grain crisis (1927–8), 31–2, 34, 36
Great Purge (1936–8), *see* purges
Gregory, P., 11, 13, 25
gross national product, 39–42, 43,
     54, 56, 60–1, 63, 65, 70–1, 76,
     79, 82
Grozny, 44
Gulag, *see* forced labour

Haimson, L., 14
Harrison, M., 27, 59
harvest, 5
  1915, 15
  1916, 16
  1920, 21
  1922, 29
  1926, 29
  1932, 54
  1945, 64
  1946, 64
health, 46, 47, 51, 70
higher education, *see* education
horses, 16
housing, 47, 69
Hunter, H., 36

import tariffs, 7
imports, 25, 27, 44; *see also* foreign
     trade
incomes, 33, 48, 57, 69, 70, 71, 74;
     *see also* wages
India, 2
industrial crops, 29, 45, 48, 67
industrial production, 38, 39, 73
  1930s, 43, 45, 50, 52, 53
  NEP, 23, 25
  post-war, 64, 65, 71
  pre-revolutionary, 7, 9
  Second World War, 60

War Communism, 21
industry
  heavy, *see* capital goods industries
  large-scale, 9, 14, 23, 24, 56
  light, *see* consumer goods
     industries
  small-scale, 9, 25, 43
industry, location of, 6, 14, 44–5, 59,
     62
infant mortality, 51, 70
inflation, 19, 24, 40, 52, 75, 77
investment, 11, 35, 36, 39, 40, 54,
     70, 73, 76
  in industry, 26, 39
  *see also* capital construction
iron and steel industry, 6, 7, 9, 11,
     23, 44, 59, 66, 69, 76; *see also*
     Magnitogorsk

Japan, 55, 72
Jasny, N., 32, 49
Jews, 63

Kahan, A., 11
Kazakhstan, 69
KGB, *see* secret police
Khanin, G. I., 35, 38, 41, 44
Khar'kov, 44
*khozraschet*, 24, 68, 75
Khrushchev, N. S., 71, 73, 77, 78
Kirov, S., 55
*kolkhozy*, *see* collective farms
Kondratiev, N., 33
*kulak*, 20, 26, 31, 34, 49; *see also*
     dekulakisation
Kursk, 62
Kuznets, S., 42

labour, 16, 19, 52
  industrial mobilisation of, 62
  unskilled, 43
labour camps, *see* forced labour
labour colonies, *see* forced labour
labour discipline, 56, 68
labour settlements, *see* forced labour
landowners, 10, 26, 21
Left Opposition, 13, 33, 34
Lend-Lease, 61, 63
Lenin, V. I., 12, 15, 18, 21, 23
Leningrad, 6, 63; *see also* Petrograd;
     St Petersburg

linen textiles, 66
literacy, 46
livestock, 14, 26, 45, 52, 53, 60, 74
living conditions, 16
living standards, *see* standard of
 living
lorries, 40, 63, 67

machine-building industry, 9, 38, 44,
 59 ; *see also* engineering industry
machine-tool industry, 15, 38, 44,
 69
Machine-Tractor Stations (MTS),
 58, 73, 78
machinery, 15, 26, 38, 40, 44, 58,
 72, 73, 77
Magnitogorsk, 44
Manchuria, 55
market equilibrium, 30, 34
market(s), 4, 6, 7, 8, 10, 11, 17, 19,
 20, 24, 32, 56, 75, 77
 collective-farm, 55, 74, 76, 78
 peasant, 52, 53
Marx, K., 17, 18, 30, 33
McKay, J. P., 13
middle class, 8, 16
migration, 31, 47, 57
Millar, J., 29, 36, 57, 58
mineral resources, 45
mining, 9, 62
money, 17, 19, 20, 21, 24, 52; *see also*
 currency; ruble
monopoly capitalism, 10, 12
Moorsteen, R., 42
Moscow, 1, 7, 14, 22, 62
munitions, *see* armaments

national income, 9, 10, 25, 61, 62–3,
 65, 72
nationalisation, 19, 20, 21
nationalities, 49, 63, 68
net national product, 56
New Economic Policy, 4, 23–37
Nicholas II, 7, 71
NKVD, *see* secret police
non-ferrous metals, 50, 59
Nove, A., 20, 58
nuclear bomb, 50, 71, 76

OGPU, *see* secret police
oil industry, 9, 14, 25, 77

Ol', P. V., 12
oligopolistic capitalism, *see* monopoly
 capitalism

peasant disturbances, 23, 53
peasant markets, *see* market(s)
peasantry, 8, 30
pensions, 47, 70
Peter the Great, 6, 71
Petrograd, 6; *see also* Leningrad; St
 Petersburg
pig-iron, 7, 11
Poland, 23
population, 1, 2, 5, 7, 9, 14, 51, 61,
 63, 79
 rural, 2
 urban, 16, 22, 47, 70
 war losses, 22, 60, 63, 64
Powell, R. P., 42
Preobrazhensky, E. A., 33, 34
price controls, 35, 52
prices, 17, 19, 24, 32, 36, 40, 52, 55,
 69, 73
 1928, 39, 40, 42
 1937, 39, 40, 42
 grain, 9, 29, 34
 retail, 28, 32, 55, 67, 75
 wholesale, 9
primary socialist accumulation, 33
productivity of labour, 34, 50, 54,
 69, 72
profit-and-loss accounting, *see*
 *khozraschet*
Provisional Government, 16, 17
purges, 48, 55

railways, 7, 8, 11, 26
rationing, 18, 19, 52, 53, 54, 61, 74
Red Army, 20, 45
reparations, 65
retail prices, *see* prices
retail trade, 24, 74
Revolution (1905), 8
Revolution (February/March 1917),
 12, 16, 17
Revolution (October/November
 1917), 12, 16, 17, 35
rolling stock, *see* railways
Rostov, 44
ruble, 11, 20, 53
Russo-Japanese War, 2, 8

St Petersburg, 6, 7, 14, 22; *see also*
    Leningrad; Petrograd
'scissors crisis', 28–9
second five-year plan, *see* five-year
    plan
Second World War, *see* World War
secret police, 81
serfdom, 6
Seton-Watson, H., 14
Shanin, T., 14
shortages, 32, 34
Siberia, 45, 50, 69
Skoropadsky, Hetman, 20
social security, 47
socialism, 3, 13, 17, 18, 21, 52, 75, 76
Sokolnikov, G., 32–3
*sovkhozy, see* state farms
space programmes, 72, 76
Spanish Civil War, 55
special settlements, *see* forced labour
specialists, 21, 52
Spulber, N., 32
Sputnik 1, 72
Stalin, I. V., 31, 34, 35, 36, 53, 54,
    58, 59, 67, 71
Stalingrad (Volgograd), 44
    Battle of, 62, 63
standard of living, 46, 47, 66, 70
    differentiation, 54
state requisitions, 53, 57
state, role in industrialisation, 3, 7,
    10, 11
state farms (*sovkhozy*), 47, 73
statistics, 4–5, 12, 38, 39
    falsification, 5, 41
Stolypin, P. A., 8, 33
    reforms, 8, 10, 13
strikes, 26
sugar, 29, 60
sugar-beet, 48
Sverdlovsk (Ekaterinburg), 44
Swaniewicz, S., 49, 50
syndicates (*sindikaty*), 9

tanks, 38, 44, 62, 63, 67
tariff policy, 11
Tarnovsky, O. I., 12
taxation, 11, 19, 24, 27, 28, 33, 36, 68
technology, 31, 43, 66, 72, 76, 77, 80
terms of trade, 27, 28, 29, 57, 58
textile industries, 6, 8, 9, 66

Timasheff, N. S., 49
timber, 50, 62
tractors, 40, 58, 67, 68, 69, 78
trade, 3, 4, 24, 25, 27, 52; *see also*
    foreign trade; retail trade
Transcaucasus, 14
transport, 23
Trotsky, L., 13, 29, 33, 34, 35
Tsarism, 12, 14
Tucker, R., 36
turnover tax, 74

Ukraine, 14, 20, 44, 45, 48
unemployment, 24, 31, 46
United States, 1, 30, 31, 39, 61, 63,
    70, 71, 79, 80
Ural-Kuznetsk combine, 76
Urals, 6, 14, 44, 45, 50

Vanag, N., 12
Virgin Lands, 69, 71
Volga region, 48
Volobuev, P. V., 12
von Laue, T., 7, 11, 15

wages, 24, 34, 46
    differentiation, 26, 54, 70, 75
    *see also* earnings; women, earnings
War Communism, 3, 17–22, 23
wheat, 67
Wheatcroft, S. G., 49
Whites, 18, 20, 21
wholesale prices, *see* prices
Witte, S., 7, 11, 32
women, 46, 64, 68–9
    earnings, 26, 69
    in agriculture, 67
    workers, 9, 16, 26, 47, 68
workers, 8, 23, 25; *see also* women,
    workers
working class, 12, 16, 17, 18, 25, 26,
    30, 54
working day, 26, 56
World War
    First, 2, 3, 15, 63, 64
    Second, 2, 41, 58–64, 74
Wrangel, General N. P., 20

Yeltsin, B., 71

Zaporozh'e, 44

# New Studies in Economic and Social History

*Titles in the series available from Cambridge University Press:*

1. M. Anderson
   *Approaches to the history of the Western family, 1500–1914*
2. W. Macpherson
   *The economic development of Japan, 1868–1941*
3. R. Porter
   *Disease, medicine, and society in England: second edition*
4. B. W. E. Alford
   *British economic performance since 1945*
5. A. Crowther
   *Social policy in Britain, 1914–1939*
6. E. Roberts
   *Women's work 1840–1940*
7. C. O'Grada
   *The great Irish famine*
8. R. Rodger
   *Housing in urban Britain 1780–1914*
9. P. Slack
   *The English poor law 1531–1782*
10. J. L. Anderson
    *Explaining long-term economic change*
11. D. Baines
    *Emigration from Europe 1815–1930*
12. M. Collins
    *Banks and industrial finance 1800–1939*
13. A. Dyer
    *Decline and growth in English towns 1400–1640*

14. R. B. Outhwaite
*Dearth, public policy and social disturbance in England, 1550–1800*

15. M. Sanderson
*Education, economic change and society in England*

16. R. D. Anderson
*Universities and elites in Britain since 1800*

17. C. Heywood
*The development of the French economy, 1700–1914*

18. R. A. Houston
*The population history of Britain and Ireland 1500–1750*

19. A. J. Reid
*Social classes and social relations in Britain 1850–1914*

20. R. Woods
*The population of Britain in the nineteenth century*

21. T. C. Barker
*The rise and rise of road transport, 1700–1990*

22. J. Harrison
*The Spanish economy*

23. C. Schmitz
*The growth of big business in the United States and Western Europe, 1850–1939*

24. R. A. Church
*The rise and decline of the British motor industry*

25. P. Horn
*Children's work and welfare, 1780–1880*

26. R. Perren
*Agriculture in depression, 1870–1940*

27. R. J. Overy
*The Nazi economic recovery 1932–1938: second edition*

28. S. Cherry
*Medical services and the hospitals in Britain, 1860–1939*

29. D. Edgerton
*Science, technology and the British industrial 'decline', 1870–1970*

30. C. A. Whatley
*The Industrial Revolution in Scotland*

31. H. E. Meller
*Towns, plans and society in modern Britain*

32. H. Hendrick
*Children, childhood and English society, 1880–1990*

33. N. Tranter
*Sport, economy and society in Britain, 1750–1914*

34. R. W. Davies
*Soviet economic development from Lenin to Khrushchev*

*Previously published as*
**Studies in Economic and Social History**

*Titles in the series available from the Macmillan Press Limited*

1. B. W. E. Alford
   *Depression and recovery? British economic growth, 1918–1939*

2. M. Anderson
   *Population change in north-western Europe, 1750–1850*

3. S. D. Chapman
   *The cotton industry in the industrial revolution: second edition*

4. M. E. Falkus
   *The industrialisation of Russia, 1700–1914*

5. J. R. Harris
   *The British iron industry, 1700–1850*

6. J. Hatcher
   *Plague, population and the English economy, 1348–1530*

7. J. R. Hay
   *The origins of the Liberal welfare reforms, 1906–1914*

8. H. McLeod
   *Religion and the working classes in nineteenth century Britain*

9. J. D. Marshall
   *The Old Poor Law 1795–1834: second edition*

10. R. J. Morris
    *Class and class consciousness in the industrial revolution, 1750–1850*

11. P. K. O'Brien
    *The economic effects of the American civil war*

12. S. B. Saul
    *The myth of the Great Depression, 1873–1896: second edition*

13.  P. L. Payne
     *British entrepreneurship in the nineteenth century*

14.  G. C. Peden
     *Keynes, the treasury and British economic policy*

15.  M. E. Rose
     *The relief of poverty, 1834–1914*

16.  J. Thirsk
     *England's agricultural regions and agrarian history, 1500–1750*

17.  J. R. Ward
     *Poverty and progress in the Caribbean, 1800–1960*

## Economic History Society

The Economic History Society, which numbers around 3,000 members, publishes the *Economic History Review* four times a year (free to members) and holds an annual conference. Enquiries about membership should be addressed to

The Assistant Secretary
Economic History Society
PO Box 70
Kingswood
Bristol
BS15 5TB

Full-time students may join at special rates.